The
HEART
of THINGS

"Wife, children, house, everything . . . the full catastrophe."
—from *Zorba the Greek*, by Nikos Kazantzakis

The

HEART

of THINGS

A Midwestern Almanac

JOHN HILDEBRAND

Wisconsin Historical Society Press

Published by the Wisconsin Historical Society Press
Publishers since 1855

wisconsin**history**.org

Photographs identified with WHi or WHS are from the Society's collections; address requests to reproduce these photos to the Visual Materials Archivist at the Wisconsin Historical Society, 816 State Street, Madison, WI 53706.

Author photo by Sharon Hildebrand

Printed in Canada

Interior design and layout by AuthorSupport.com

Cover design by Percolator Graphic Design

18 17 16 15 14 1 2 3 4 5

Library of Congress Cataloging-in-Publication Data

Hildebrand, John.
 The heart of things : a Midwestern almanac / John Hildebrand.
     pages cm
  ISBN 978-0-87020-672-6 (hardback) — ISBN 978-0-87020-673-3 (ebook)
 1. Wisconsin—Social life and customs—Anecdotes. 2. Wisconsin—Social life and customs—Calendars. 3. Middle West—Social life and customs—Anecdotes. 4. Middle West—Social life and customs—Calendars. 5. Country life—Calendars. I. Title.
  F581.6.H55 2014
  977—dc23
                                2014018398

∞ The paper used in this publication meets the minimum requirements of the American National Standard for Information Sciences—Permanence of Paper for Printed Library Materials, ANSI Z39.48-1992.

This book is for
Rosemary and Cecelia

Contents

Introduction

IN THE MOVIES, the Midwest is the place we're forever leaving—for big cities on the coast or more open spaces farther west—to begin our real lives. It's a line or two of the backstory, an exterior shot: cornfields, a water tower against a blue sky receding rapidly in a rearview mirror on the highway to skyscrapers and romance. There's a reason why screenwriters gave both Annie Hall and the Jack Dawson character in *Titanic* a Chippewa Falls address: to signal their innocence in contrast to slicker, more worldly types. I lived in Chippewa Falls for a time and know movie references to be a mixed blessing. Visiting other parts of the country, I'd feel obliged to meet expectations, to act simpler and more earnest than I normally act, to play Jack Dawson to anyone's Rose. Irony? I'd say, looking around with a big grin. What's that?

Time and place might be the coordinates, the latitude and longitude, by which we chart our position in the world, but *things* are what we remember. *Where was I then?* is just another way of asking *Who was I then?* And the answer is inevitably tied to some ordinary object—not the big ticket items but a solid, physical detail around which the intangible clings: the summer of fireflies, the winter the cow shed collapsed, that early autumn the garden froze. At least that's how I remember—one thing leading to another, and somewhere an idea tangled in the middle.

This isn't a journal of any particular year, not a report of events as they occurred, but a record of things that grew in reflection over time. Most of these short essays were written over a seven-year period when I wrote a regular column for *Wisconsin Trails* magazine. Having never written a column before, I looked for models, and the best I could find were the essays E.B. White wrote for *Harper's* in the 1930s and '40s. It was White who described the essayist as "a self-liberated man, sustained by the childish belief that everything he thinks about, everything that happens to him, is of general interest." That made perfect sense to me.

The job came with three restrictions: my column had to be seasonal, it couldn't run much over seven hundred words, and it had to be centered in the Midwest. On the whole, I tried to be celebratory without falling into the trap of local color where picturesque natives inhabit the Land Time Forgot. I've never believed that living in one place means being one thing all the time, condemned like Minnie Pearl to wear the same hat for every performance. Life is more complicated than that.

My grandmother's view of the world resembled the Saul Steinberg cartoon of New York City in which civilization ends at the Hudson River and the landscape beyond trails off into a featureless steppe. Only in the case of my grandmother, a life-long Chicagoan, the known world began at The Loop and ended a little north of O'Hare Airport. Beyond those venues, she didn't much care. Parochial in every sense of the word, she took her news from the *Chicago Tribune,* an archdiocesan weekly, and the neighbor woman in the apartment above hers whose daily phone conversations only confirmed my grandmother's insular sense of the world. On the rare occasions she ventured from home, it was inevitably to a place that served a "good prime rib" and a decent Irish whiskey. The old woman knew what she liked.

It's a tricky notion, this idea of home—and easily mistaken for a pigeonhole. More useful, I think, is the concept of home range, which isn't a single spot on the map but several spots and all the space in between. If a wildlife biologist clamped a radio collar around my neck and tracked my movements over time, he'd eventually draw a convex polygon not so different in shape from my grandmother's world, a territory defined by the familiar outposts of home, work, and play. Most of life's dramas play out not at the ends of the earth, but in all the usual places. So that's the geography I've staked out in these essays—places where I discovered not only what I like, but also what matters. And if I bounce from one spot to the next, it's always with the sweet belief that wherever I am at the moment lies deep in the very heart of things.

JANUARY

Winter People

I LOVE THIS TIME OF YEAR when the cold settles in and a long-shadowed light falls through the woods. The county roads are deserted and the quiet goes on forever. The country has emptied of summer people—with the exception of myself. A winter person by temperament, I don't book a flight south when the snow flies but head north to my cabin.

The first order of business is shoveling a path to the cabin door. Once inside, I can still see my breath. Coming to the cabin in winter always reminds me of the scene in *Doctor Zhivago* when the good doctor breaks into the family's ice-encrusted *dacha* to wait out the revolution writing poetry while an unseen balalaika plucks out the opening notes of "Somewhere My Love." When I hit the breaker switch, the radio, which is tuned to WOJB broadcasting from the Lac Courte Oreilles Reservation, fills the room with the deep, accusing baritone of Johnny Cash. I stuff the woodstove with birch logs and kindling, strike a match, and go someplace warm.

At the supper club down the road, the owner remembers not only my name but the brand of beer I drink. I'll slip onto a stool, unzip my parka, and watch whatever everyone else is watching on the overhead TV. I like to imagine that I fit in here—and I do, if fitting in means being privy to township gossip or allowed to voice an opinion on the DNR. In truth, it's hard to pick out summer people from residents in the winter when everybody wears puffy coats and roots for the same NFL franchise. Still, in the battle of roots, wintering over trumps the weekend visit no matter how many years you've been coming north.

It's a difference in equity. The cottager invests disposable income and even sweat into his lodgey retreat, but not his life. That's why the supper club owner, who took out a mortgage on this place only a few years ago, is already home for the night while I'm just killing time—one more flighty snowbird.

After Labor Day, locals are more than happy to reclaim the lakes and woods they've had to share all summer. It's as if a noisy bunch of house guests or extended family has finally left and normal life can resume. And yet the summer crowd underpins the local economy while deer hunting and weekend incursions by snowmobilers keep it going through the cold months. This symbiotic relationship works for everyone concerned as long as a balance is struck between residents and transients. Too many permanent residents and the North Woods becomes a suburb, too few and it turns into a winter ghostland.

My friend the tax assessor tracks inflation at 17 percent all over northern Wisconsin. Sometimes I'll go along for the ride, just "kickin' tires" and getting a feel for the market. One cold January we drove his red Jeep to a pretty resort town on Lake Superior. The sun was going down as deer fed in the bare orchards above the town. Descending to the main street, my friend pointed to a row of gingerbread houses, all lacy bargeboard at the gable ends and drifted deep in snow.

"Look at that. Half-a-million-dollar houses and no tracks to the doors and driveways unplowed."

Nearly all the houses were like that. Darkness fell and not a single light came on. If a Russian poet had broken into one of these *dachas* to write some verse, he'd be working in the dark.

We sat on barstools in the only tavern still open listening to an older man who'd grown up in the town when its fortunes were tied to whitefish and lake trout instead of tourism. He complained that while the influx of summer residents had greatly increased the value of his own home, it did so at an unexpected price. The younger generation, those with school-age kids, had largely moved away, relocating in a less picturesque, more working-class town a short drive to the south.

"Back when I was a kid, a million years ago, there were kids on every street corner. We'd get together for ball games. Now young families can't afford to live here."

The old man made his lost childhood sound as if it had been spent in some mythic village on the sea like long-ago Hamlin before the ratcatcher came to town.

Church Supper

ON THE COLDEST NIGHT in January, the head cook ducks out of the kitchen to assess the crowd lined up in the school cafeteria. If the line ends at the double doors, all is well. But if the line snakes out the doors and past the low-set water fountain and into the hallway where racks have been placed for people to hang their heavy coats, then he'll need to add another sixty pounds of Alaskan pollack to the pot. Other ingredients for the fish boil can be prepared ahead of time, but the mainstay, the pollack, has to be thawed on the spot. Hence the frequent scouting trips. The cook jogs back to the kitchen.

"Father," he says to a man in the back of the kitchen, "I don't mean to rush you, but we could really use some more fish."

Reverend Eugene Klink bends over the cafeteria sink in the same posture I've seen him bent over the altar during the offertory at Mass and for somewhat the same purpose: to feed the multitude. Here he holds a solid block of frozen pollack under tap water until the fish is multiplied into a handful of limp fillets. The fillets go into a boiling cauldron of seasoned brine along with a basket of peeled onions and another of red potatoes. Three minutes later, when the cook and his assistants hoist the steaming baskets from the cauldron, a heat wave runs through the room as if the kitchen had suddenly crash-landed in some equatorial jungle where the undergrowth was thick with garlic, onions, and oregano.

For twenty years, Immaculate Conception Parish has held a New England–style fish boil every other Friday night between the end of January and whenever Easter falls. This six-week period roughly coincides with the Liturgical season of Lent, that gray time of self-denial and giving up, but it's hard to see exactly what patrons of the fish boil give up, unless it's cooking for the night. What they get, beside fish, potatoes, carrots, coleslaw, and a little ice cream cup, is a break from winter doldrums, a chance to cheer up after the Christmas decorations come down. Who needs a fancy restaurant when you can go to an elementary school cafeteria and eat wholesome, no-frills food? Some customers (those who don't take off their coats) order carryout, but they miss out on the chance to relive that thrilling moment from childhood when you look up from your lunch tray and wonder where to sit.

As a parishioner, I've been a regular sucker for fund-raisers—selling concessions at the school's football games, guilt-tripped into buying overpriced popcorn or pizzas or whatever—but I actually like the fish boil. I'll come the night before to help with preparations: three hundred pounds of carrots and red potatoes, another two hundred pounds of yellow onions. For some reason, the men gravitate toward the onions, cutting them at arm's length, while the women peel the carrots with a wrist motion like dealing cards. As they work, the women compare notes on the competition, the suppers offered at neighboring parishes like Saint Olaf and Holy Rosary that compete for the Friday night crowd. "Those others," says a carrot-peeler, "are *deep*-fried."

Most of the time, I work the fish boil as a dishwasher, which is the kitchen equivalent of playing left field. There's little pressure and plenty of time to look around. Despite the hothouse heat, I catch an occasional breeze from the open casement window above the sink, and there are periodic lulls between stacks of dirty dishes. The other volunteers—ticket-takers, busboys, dishwashers, fish-thawers—are people I see the rest of the year only in their professional guises as dentist or salesman or priest. And it's reassuring to see them in a different light, all of us wearing the same flimsy plastic apron with a paper nametag. Only the cook crew are set apart by their pinstriped cloth aprons embroidered *I.C. Fish Boil* and no name tag because everyone knows who they are. The head cook, a locksmith, has done this for twenty years. As the customers trickle down toward the end of the evening, the cook crew pass around a few cans of beer that have been cooling in the walk-in freezer for just this moment. It's the grace after the meal.

Muskrats

DNR Outdoor Report for January 22: Muskrats are again being reported for frightening ice anglers. They are merely investigating holes in the ice and perhaps getting a breath of fresh air. When they surface inside a dark shack or tent, they may even mistakenly think they have arrived home.

MUSKRATS? SURFACING AGAIN? Try to imagine the scene: not the angler's surprise at a small, wet rodent hauling itself from a hole in the ice to share his small space but the deeper shock and disappointment of the rodent who's swum through darkness thinking he's home only to realize at the last minute that he's not.

I know that feeling. It usually surfaces in dreams that follow a move, weeks after the boxes have been unpacked but long before the mental transfer of title takes place when you think to yourself: This is it now. Home.

How long does that take? At least until you're able to maneuver around the house at night without switching on the lights. When your feet can feel their way around corners or mount the stairs without you holding the wall, that's the point where I'd say you've safely arrived home. Until then, however, the mind has a way of picking up the scent of the old place and breathlessly crossing mountains and oceans to get there.

When I first moved to Wisconsin, I had reoccurring dreams about making my way back to a log cabin I'd built north of the Outer Range of mountains in Alaska only to find it buried beneath a subdivision. (In fact the cabin was crumbling back into the woods, and you didn't have to be Freud to understand why I'd invented a different scenario.) Given enough time, the Midwestern landscape replaced the Alaskan one in my subconscious, and I started dreaming about my wife's family farm, especially the ragged field my father-in-law called the Night Pasture because the cows would go there in the evening after being milked. All these dreams were a form of time travel. They were also, it strikes me now, a last glance backwards in a long good-bye.

But to return to ice fishing. Once a year I like to stand on frozen water and fish without a boat. The last time was on Blockhouse Lake, where my friend Jim drilled six black portals through the ice with a power auger; then we lowered shiner-baited treble hooks into the holes and waited for something to happen. Nothing much did. Snow began falling in a spangled, Christmas-card sort of way and there wasn't a muskrat in sight. Jim gestured across the lake to the house he and his wife had built on a point, though I couldn't see it through the white pines. That had been his idea, leaving a screen of pines so the house wouldn't show from the lake. It was Jim's way of being unobtrusive, knowing people prefer to see pine trees rather than lake homes. He and Audrey had done something I didn't think possible past a certain age: changed their lives by changing addresses. After retirement, they moved three hours north to a place where neither of them knew anyone. What does it take to make a home? Not much: some familiar furniture, a set of dishes, a few pictures on the wall. Jim and Audrey understood that home isn't so much a building as a web of connections and obligations, so they did volunteer work, got involved in local politics, and landed feet first in the community.

The spring after we'd gone ice fishing, I read a small item in the newspaper about a forest fire that burned one hundred acres along Blockhouse Lake and three structures, only one of which qualified as a permanent dwelling, and that was Jim and Audrey's house. The fire began with a blown transformer and then, pushed along by stiff winds, had leaped a bay and ignited the pines that Jim had been loath to cut. It moved so fast that Jim had only enough time to rescue his laptop and a dog before the house caught fire and burned to the ground. Everything else was lost.

I visited them the next year after they'd rebuilt on the same site but with a different floor plan and no screen of pines. I asked Audrey if the new place felt like home.

"It took a while because everything was new. Every object had a learning curve to it, a new look and a different feel. But with the kids' help we decorated the house and started new memories, so it seems now that yes, this is home."

Then she added: "I still dream about the old place. And sometimes in the middle of the night I'll turn left to go into the bathroom, where it used to be, and find myself in the office."

Native Son

I WAS LOOKING for another chair. Three of us had snagged a table in a hotel bar, all chrome and mirrors, but came up a chair short. So I shoehorned through the crowd, attendees of a Modern Language Association conference, men and women in dark suits and little black dresses who had earlier presented papers on "Historicizing Ida Lupino" or "Mario Lanza and the Third World" and were now drinking flavored vodka and looking smart . . . as would I once I had a place to sit. Finally I located an empty chair at an otherwise occupied table and asked if I might take it.

Half a dozen faces looked up and studied me as if I was a sentence that needed deconstructing. At last a small man with a trim Van Dyke spoke up, "You're from the Midwest, aren't you?"

When I asked how he knew, the man smiled.

"Because you *asked*."

Grinning like an idiot, I bore the chair away feeling somehow diminished, no longer a man of the world but one more bumpkin fallen off the turnip truck, my suit suddenly flecked with hay.

Sometimes I get tired of Midwest nice. No. I get tired of other people's assumptions about the Midwest. When a "Midwestern" character in a novel speaks like Ole or Lena, I cringe. Sometimes I wish Garrison Keillor and the whole humble population of Lake Woebegone would set up shop on Long Island. Why not let Montauk or one of Hamptons be the Land Time Forgot for a change? See how they like it.

In Hollywood, place always plays a role in the backstory. If the West is where we're going in the movies, then the Midwest is where we're *from*. It's Bedford Falls or Mr. Deed's hometown or it's *Happy*

Days or *That Seventies Show*. It's never here-and-now but a place tucked safely in the past, a distant land where people still smile and say "Please" and "Thank you" and "You're very welcome" but lack street smarts—the poor dolts—which makes them vulnerable to more sophisticated, ironic types like my bearded interlocutor at the bar. Perhaps I should have bitten off one of his ears. That would have made him look at the Midwest in a totally new and unexpected light.

Movies aside, I don't believe geography is fate. Where you're from doesn't necessarily dictate who you are. I've lived in half a dozen states before ending up here and found people no less dependable in each. So much of what the nation ascribes to the Midwest as a whole—a lack of pretense, a respect for physical labor, a tendency toward understatement—are rural values, hardly changed since the late eighteenth century when J. Hector St. John de Crevecoeur, a transplanted Frenchman, codified them in *Notes from an American Farmer*. As the number of people living on farms dwindles (in Wisconsin it's less than 3 percent), do those qualities transfer to the rest of us by osmosis? I don't think so.

A few years ago, I lost a friend who embodied just about every trait we associate with the Midwest. He grew up on a farm in a large family. Even after moving to a city, he loved being in the country. He loved to hunt. He was a veteran and a family man and he spoke softly and deliberately and with an understated sense of humor that put everyone at ease.

His name was Joe Bee Xiong, and he was born in Xieng Khouang Province in northern Laos. He didn't reach Wisconsin until his late teens, having already experienced much of the world. To call him a strictly a Midwesterner, a product of our native soil, would be to flatter ourselves.

Going Outside

ON THE COLDEST, darkest nights of winter, I'll sink into the big Morris chair beside my fireplace and reread *The Worst Journey in the World*, Apsley Cherry-Garrard's firsthand account of the ill-fated British Antarctic Expedition of 1910–1913. I love the author's Edwardian locutions, the mixture of formality and stiff-upper-lip understatement that marked that generation of polar explorers. After a few pages, the fireplace insert begins to seem like a blubber stove and the dark beyond my living room window like the impenetrable darkness of McMurdo Sound. By chapter's end I'll hunt up some excuse to go outside.

Maybe the dog needs walking. Or the wood box is low. Maybe somebody ought to confirm those wild rumors that the moon is full. Whatever, I really must be going. Who can stay inside when a winter night makes even a trip around the block seem expeditionary, the cold itself a heroic destination?

January marks the height of the tourist season in the Antarctic, when dozens of cruise ships bring visitors to see penguins and an antipodal sun that never sets. But sailing to 90° south isn't necessary to experience polar travel. The same night in Wisconsin can be colder and certainly darker than in Antarctica, where it's summer and blazing sunlight twenty-four hours a day. Beyond a certain threshold, cold is cold. I've been more miserable trudging up Wisconsin Avenue at ten degrees into a cold wet wind than I have riding a snowmobile across the desert-dry Arctic coastal plain at thirty below. The difference was gear.

The success of Roald Amundsen's expedition to the South Pole, as opposed to the tragic failure of Captain Robert Falcon Scott's, is often attributed to the Norwegians' better gear. Taking their cue from Netsilik Inuit, they traveled by dog team and ski and wore reindeer parkas with wolf fur ruffs that wouldn't frost while the British, man-hauling their supplies over the ice, alternately sweated and froze in cotton windbreakers worn over woolens. My own cold-weather gear spends most of the year in a cardboard box in the closet waiting for just such a night as this. If it's really, really cold, I'll put on nylon wind pants, boot-pacs with Thinsulate liners, GI gauntlet mittens over wool gloves, a watch cap, and the sort of down parka favored by both North Slope oil-rig workers and urban hip-hop artists. At this point I fill the hallway.

Explorers fall back on words like *grandeur* and *austere* and *sublime* to describe the blank polar landscape. "Indeed a man may realize," wrote Cherry-Garrard, "how beautiful this world can be, and how clean." What winter bestows on the familiar landscape are solitude and a sense of limits. One travels the neighborhood alone and as self-contained as a moonwalker lumbering through the cold night of outer space, the only sound the crunch of snow underfoot. The point of going outside is to remind ourselves of the thin layer of technology that allows us to largely forget that it's winter.

Winter camping is a sure cure for such complacency. Some years ago I skied through the Chequamegon-Nicolet National Forest dragging a small sled on which I'd piled my tent and other supplies. Wrapped in a mummy bag that night, I had trouble falling asleep because my breath kept crystallizing against the sloping side of the tent and falling back in my face in miniature snow showers. Later, after I'd managed to drift into sleep, I woke with a start because my left arm had gone numb and wouldn't move.

It felt like marble. I stifled a scream once I realized that my arm wasn't frozen; I'd simply rolled over in my sleep and cut off the circulation. But for the rest of that night I couldn't help thinking of poor Scott's party freezing to death at the bottom of the earth.

"Great God! This is an awful place and terrible enough for us to have labored to it without the reward of priority," a disappointed Scott wrote in his diary after reaching the Pole on January 17, 1912, a month after Amundsen had won the prize. A recent book by a scientist at the National Oceanic and Atmospheric Administration examined weather records for the Antarctic and concluded that the British ran into far worse conditions that anyone had reason to expect for that time of year. Even better gear might not have saved them.

I'm not going to the Pole tonight, only around the block. Fully geared up, I'll whistle for the dog and harness him to the leash. Then I'll quietly inform my wife where we're headed, repeating Captain Lawrence Oates's final words as he stepped from the tent into a raging blizzard: "I am just going outside and may be some time."

FEBRUARY

On the Edge

IN GEOGRAPHY TEXTS, one proof given that the world is round shows a figure on a seashore watching the approach of a ship. Because of the earth's curvature, the ship appears in stages: smokestack, main deck, and finally hull. But the proof requires a ship. Stand on the shore of Lake Superior in winter when the ore boats are gone, and the world looks exceedingly flat—flat and white—and it ends sharply at the horizon.

For several years I've driven to Lake Superior in February to ski across the ice at night with a thousand other oddballs. Book Across the Bay is a ten-kilometer race that runs from Ashland to Washburn across frozen Chequamegon Bay with the course marked by hundreds of flickering luminaries. I began skiing the race after a series of mild winters made it one of the only reliable places to find snow. But even in heavy snow years, I keep coming back for reasons hard to explain. By midwinter, the cold and dark can start to feel like a single element—*coldanddark*—in which one's life is suspended. Candlelight skiing breaks the inertia by turning what is otherwise depressing, namely the cold and the dark, into a source of fun.

At twilight the racers assemble on the ice below the Hotel Chequamegon just down from the old ore dock. There is a brief, Turneresque moment at sunset when the clouds turn black against a pearly sky and the far shore is still visible as a line of blue hills. Then the light goes out and the cold becomes sharper. A pistol shot, and the line surges forward with a great scuttling of skis and poles. At first I'm carried along by the crowd's momentum until I settle into a pace that keeps me out of the way of the serious skiers but ahead of the snowshoers and dawdlers. Among the skiers, there are those who skate and those who stride. A skater myself, I swing my arms and legs in rhythm to my own breathing. That's what you hear in the thick of the crowd—heavy breathing, the sound of everyone inhaling and exhaling together without a word exchanged. It's as if we were all linked to the same circadian rhythms and nightfall had been the cue for triggering a mass migration over the ice—like barren ground caribou or suicidal lemmings.

The course doesn't head straight for the lights of Washburn but makes a dogleg toward the mouth of the bay before veering back to shore. If not for the dark, I'd be able to confirm the earth is a globe by watching skiers disappear in stages over the horizon— except that the horizon itself has disappeared. Instead, I'm skiing more or less by feel. The luminaries show the way but not the condition of the snow underfoot or if a frost heave or a bare patch of ice lies ahead, so I just concentrate on staying upright. Far ahead, a light glows brighter and brighter until it becomes a lantern-lit tent—the halfway point. Volunteers hand out orange slices and paper cups of warm water, though the serious racers never stop here. By the time I return to the race, the crowd has moved on, and I find myself alone on what seems the dark side of the moon. Away from the lights of Ashland, the night sky is so jammed with constellations that the luminaries seem an extension of Orion's Belt. Passing a blank stretch where some candles have guttered out, I wonder what might happen if I miss a turn. (So far as I know, nobody has.) Would I notice the line where ice ends and open water begins or would I, intoxicated by stars, blithely keep skiing until I fall off the edge?

The thought is broken by a *whumpf* and explosion overhead. The rocket signals that the first skier has crossed the finish line. More important from my perspective, the fireworks reveal that I'm not alone out here. A ragged line of skiers, previously obscured by darkness, has suddenly materialized in the shadowy light, all of us moving steadily toward shore and a blazing bonfire that marks our return to the known world.

Compost

WE KEEP A COMPOST PILE in the far corner of the backyard. Is this legal? I couldn't say, but it's the perfect Something-for-Nothing scheme. You toss Nothing—vegetable peelings, coffee grounds, melon rinds—into a fenced enclosure, throw a little dirt on the pile, and, after a few months decomposing, it becomes Something: good black soil that can be used as top-dressing on the garden. The invigorated garden grows more vegetables that produce more peelings and turn into more compost . . . and so on and so forth, world without end, amen. The beauty of this alchemy is that it's free and requires no middleman except the person who carries the small tub of kitchen scraps from the back door to the compost pile, which most nights is me.

In summer this is a pleasant task, and sometimes I'll linger with a pitchfork to sift through the compost for nightcrawlers. But in winter it's a different story—a tightrope walk through the snow and ice balancing a tub of slop. The trees are leafless and the garden lies buried in a way that looks permanent so connecting it to some future bounty seems unimaginable. In winter a trip to the compost pile is one more *memento mori* in a dreary season of loss.

Only the dog looks forward to these trips, barreling out the back door and across the snow at full bark. *WUHH! . . . WUHH! . . . WUHH!* The dog has taken a proprietary interest in the compost pile. He regards it as a sort of unburied bone and every night makes a frontal assault on the pile in case a crow is lurking atop it. There never is, but the happy memory of a time when there was a crow and the dog sent it flapping and cawing into the air is enough for him to nightly reenact Pickett's charge. *WUHH!* ... *WUHH!* ... *WUHH!*

On this particular night, a full moon made the white yard appear lit from below. Lagging behind as usual, I heard the dog's rebel yell lower into a growl. Ahead, the dog had something in its mouth, something about the size of the neighbor's cat, and was vigorously shaking it back and forth. I ran to the pile, leaving behind a trail of spilled peelings. The dog stood over the animal, which was not a cat, thank God, but a dead opossum.

The dog, a poodle mix, isn't a natural-born killer, content to live and let live with most creatures, though he once dispatched a pair of black hens that he mistook for the dreaded crows. He seemed pleased then despite my wife's profuse apologies to the chickens' owner, and he seemed pleased now as he hovered over the recumbent opossum and acted as if I should be as well. But it's hard to feel hunky-dory about any animal that dies in your backyard, even if it's wild and uninvited. As a hunter, I rationalize killing animals by eating them, though neither the dog nor I were interested in a meal of opossum. Instead, I felt what children feel when confronting a dead animal for the first time: curiosity. The opossum lay on its side, a scaly pink rat's tail at one end and a pale, conical head at the other that sharpened to a point, teeth exposed in a foiled grin. Apart from bell-ringing ugliness, all the opossum signified now was common mortality, a creature once alive as you or I and now dead.

There was the question of what to do with the corpse. As flesh, it was not a candidate for the compost pile, and I went to the garage to get a shovel so I could dispose of the body in the trash. On the way, I fetched my son, home from college, in case he wanted to see a dead opossum. When we returned, the body was gone. The dog and I were flummoxed but not the college student. The opossum, he observed dryly, had "played possum" on us, whereupon he walked back to the warm house. I soon followed, leaving the dog to ponder this mystery alone.

There's some dispute among biologists as to whether opossums consciously feign death (thanatosis) or have an involuntary reflex (tonic immobility) that causes a temporary coma. Personally, I hope it's not a conscious trick—and not just because the dog and I were bamboozled. I'd like to imagine the opossum's own great surprise at its resurrection and the rejoicing this miraculous return might cause among its opossum kin and any others looking for signs the dark season is losing its grip.

Farm Girl

MY WIFE ONCE WON Reserve Grand Champion at the Olmsted County Fair for a lamb she raised as a 4-H project. She was twelve at the time; her father gave her the lamb in late winter and for months she kept it groomed and fed and made sure the straw bedding in its stall was fresh. Then in the summer, on the last night of the fair, she steered the lamb around the livestock auction ring, keeping one hand under its chin and another on its rump, so implement dealers and feed store owners and Jaycees could bid on it. By now the five-month-old lamb weighed as much as she did, and keeping it broadside to the stands was a contest of wills. But she managed. The auctioneer shouted into the microphone, his flat vowels and folksy manner coaxing up the price. There was a round of applause when a savings and loan paid $160 for the Reserve Grand Champion so it could declare a dividend of chops and roasts. The money went into a savings account for the unforeseeable future, that place where we currently reside. When I asked my wife if she'd felt sad selling her pet lamb, she said no. And it wasn't a pet.

You can be married to someone for decades only to realize that deep within lies a person you hardly know. The farm my wife grew up on was a diverse enterprise where three generations lived under one roof and raised dairy cows, beef cattle, sheep, hogs, chickens, and horses, not to mention several cash crops and an orchard. That place no longer exists. It'd become a shoestring operation by the time we married, with a scattering of outbuildings that had outlived their original functions like the old sheep shed I tore down one summer to build a corral fence. I ended up writing a book about the farm partly to fill in the blanks in family history and partly to understand my wife. I interviewed uncles and aunts, read agricultural history, and pored over old photographs—but the information I gleaned was all after the fact. What a childhood on the farm was like during the 1950s and '60s remained left to the imagination.

Long after the book was published, I was rummaging around in the dresser drawer and found a leather-bound pocket diary with my wife's name written on the flyleaf: *Sharon O'Neill, Rt 3.* Each small, lined page covered two calendar days, not much room for introspection. But emotions aren't what an eleven-year-old records; instead it's day-to-day events that seem extraordinary because each day is freshly minted. The entries begin in 1965, a year before the diarist's triumph at the county fair.

JANUARY 8

Real Real Real Cold. Turned colder than ice. And there was a lot of ice too. The creek was froze. The yard was slippery. Everything was covered with ice. Dad went to town.

JANUARY 10

Went to church in morning. Had dinner in school. Potluck is what we had. It was lots of fun. At night a skunk was around the house, went under the porch. Mom got sick of smell.

JANUARY 11

Got colder. Got up at 8:00 and Dad had to wake us up. We finally had music but not square dancing. Instead had singing. We skated after school. Took the sled.

Any childhood feels self-contained when you're in the midst of it. A farm, though, really is a separate world made up of concentric rings—house, yard, school, church, and, on the distant horizon, town. A child moves easily from one sphere of influence to another because they all, apart from town, reinforce each other, populated as they are with relatives and neighbors and others who only wish you well. Much is made of the independence of the American farmer living spread across the countryside on separate quarter-sections; less is made of the social institutions—school, church, township government—that bound rural people together and made such isolation tolerable. Between the O'Neills and their neighbors across the road, the Sheehans, a dozen or more children make the half-mile march to school each day. The new red brick school at the end of the road is directly across from the old one-room school that now serves as the town hall. It's the peculiar fate of Midwestern schoolhouses to end their days either as a granary or the seat of local government.

FEBRUARY 4

It warmed up to 4 above. Then it got windy. When we got home from school had to chase the sheep in because some are going to have lambs.

FEBRUARY 6

Went to catechism. Last night the wind howled like mad and I woke up about 4 times. One time it was because the wind stopped and it was so quiet. Got much warmer and melted all the snow.

FEBRUARY 7

It froze during the night and Boy is it Slippery! Yes it's slippery. All is a solid mass of ice. Went to L City. Mom won't cross river. Went out for supper.

February is such a cold, dreary month, at least for adults, but there's little sign of boredom or confinement in the diary. Weather is almost always the major event. Compared to the televised troubles on the evening news, a snowfall or an ice storm is palpably real. It casts the day in a peculiar light and alters the landscape in a way that opens up new possibilities—downhill sledding and ice-skating on a frozen pond—without one ever leaving the farm. There are still chores to be done, some of which—like chasing sheep or gathering eggs—are indistinguishable from play except that they're "useful," a term that means you're holding up your part of the bargain.

FEBRUARY 11

Went back to school. In the morning I finished the Valentine Box. It's cute. Had our party. Before going home it started to snow a little.

FEBRUARY 12

It snowed 14 to 18 inches!!!!!!!!!! Drifts everywhere, at least 3 to 4 ft. deep. Kids got school off. Dad was plowing like mad. Went sliding. Had fun!!

FEBRUARY 13

Had no catechism because of the snow. Went out and jumped in a bunch of drifts. Went up to Sheehan's to get eggs. Missy followed. I caught her & sent her home.

Missy is a black and gray collie mix, and like every other living thing on the farm she has a job. Hers is being the farm dog, a position that requires barking diligently when anyone new drives into the yard. It means keeping other animals in their place by whatever means necessary, like chasing a calf that's slipped through the pasture fence or wringing the neck of a raccoon that's moved into the barn. It means accompanying children everywhere within the boundaries of the farm, but it does not mean crossing the road to the Sheehans', who have their own farm dog, or ranging freely over the countryside, inclinations that can get a dog shot.

FEBRUARY 23

Getting excited about tomorrow.

FEBRUARY 24

Went to Central, got off the bus, found Anita and went to her locker. Had tests, films. Ate lunch. Had entertainment. Got out of school. Had a lamb.

FEBRUARY 25

Was real tired about yesterday in the morning. When we got to school, Mrs. Madson said we couldn't settle down. Rita and I checked the sheep. The lamb from yesterday died.

The Scottish poet Edwin Muir, raised on a croft in the Orkney Islands, once observed, "A farm is such a carnival of life and death there is no wonder it should frighten a child." Maybe. But a childhood on the farm is also preparation for the harsh realities of life, one of which is that nothing lasts. So it's not surprising that the lamb's passing made less of an impression on the diarist than the prospect of an hour-long bus ride to Central Junior High. The visit would offer a glimpse of what's to come, which won't be on the farm but in one town or another. Instead of Mrs. Madson's combined fifth and sixth grade stocked with familiar faces, school in town will be made up of kids who don't live on farms and regard those who do as "hayseeds" and "hicks." It will mark the end of thinking that the world is a small place inhabited solely by people who wish you well. But all that's in the future. For now, in the diary, it's still February 1965, and there's plenty of time to believe the life you've always known, this private kingdom of animals and useful people, will go on forever.

FEBRUARY 26

It's finally Friday. Seemed like a long week. Started and finished my diorama. Had square dancing with the other room. Had only two classes in school. Day seemed to fly by.

FEBRUARY 27

Went to catechism. Handed in report cards. Dad went to sale. It was real nice. Snow melted. Bridge overflowed. Water rushed down from the cow-yard.

FEBRUARY 28

Had triplet lambs last night. Went to church. It was nice today too. In the afternoon we thought March would come in like a lamb. We were holding lambs all afternoon.

A Sense of Snow

THIRTY-ODD YEARS AGO when I moved to Wisconsin, more or less permanently, I thought I had a pretty good fix on the state. With an empty house to furnish, I drove to many farm auctions and acquired a great deal of mismatched furniture that turned my home into an aesthetic puzzle. At one of those auctions, the furniture's former owner was an elderly farmer in striped overalls with an enlarged thyroid gland hanging from his neck like an eggplant. First impressions are important, so when a friend asked about my new life in Wisconsin, I replied that the state seemed largely populated by old people with goiters. Tourists and travel writers often make sweeping assumptions about a new locale and pass this nonsense off as *sense of place*. "The native, by contrast," according to UW–Madison geographer Yi-Fu Tuan, "has a complex attitude derived from his immersion in the totality of his environment. The visitor's viewpoint, being simple, is easily stated."

How true. The longer I live here, the harder it is to say exactly what *here* means. From one state to another, we shop at the same stores, eat the same fast food, listen to the same braying voices on the radio as if all DJs graduated from the same frenetic school of broadcasting. But one aspect of place that remains fixed for me is weather. Wisconsin is a place where winter matters, where cold and snow prevail at least three months of the year. This assumption has come under assault in the last decade, however, as meteorologists beam over "record high" temperatures or assure us that we've "dodged a bullet" when the next blizzard slams into Ontario instead of us. Some winters my cross-country skis emerge from the closet for only a few weekends, while the snowshoes on the wall have become purely *objets d'art*. I don't feel cheated by the lack of snow, I feel displaced.

A winter without snow sounds different, for one thing. There's nothing to muffle the sound of cars passing on the street, no tanklike roar when the city plow makes a sweep. And the quality of light is different because there's nothing to reflect it back into the sky so that the nights are even darker. Without snow, the backyard is no longer a palimpsest of animal tracks to be read each morning, and the frost sinks deeper into the garden soil because there's no insulating cover. Against these losses, the weatherman's cheerful comments seem pretty thin.

The old notion of climate change was flying south when winter dragged on too long. Now it means getting in my car and driving north to look for cross-country snow. Some winters, the skiing begins just north of Highway 8; other years a trip to the Lake Superior snowbelt is in order. In February 2000 I drove to Hayward, where the American Birkebeiner ski race had been canceled for the first time in its history. Instead of skating down Main Street to the finish line, elite skiers from around the world tiptoed among the rain puddles. The short-term effects of this kind of climate change can be measured in lost revenues for businesses that depend on snow. The long-term effect is that you end up living in a different place.

It's easy to sentimentalize winters past, to remember only snow days and cold snaps and the landscape as a Currier and Ives print. But our winters are, in fact, getting shorter and milder. Annual records kept since 1855 of freeze and thaw dates on Madison's Lake Monona reveal that the duration of ice cover on the lake has been steadily shrinking. In the 1970s, when I first moved to Wisconsin, the lake's surface was frozen an average of one hundred days a year, almost two weeks less than the average a century earlier. But in the last decade, ice cover has shrunk to an average of eighty days, which is hardly surprising given that nine of the ten warmest years on record have occurred since 1990. And while average winter temperatures have gone up statewide, the greatest increase has been in the north.

I live in west-central Wisconsin, which historically lies within the transition zone between tall grass prairie and oak savanna to the west and mixed hardwood forests to the north. The flora and fauna that define those zones are largely determined by weather: sunlight, precipitation, and temperature. Milder winters will mean more oak forests and grasslands but less of what we think of as the North Woods. The remnant boreal forests of spruce and fir along Lake Superior will almost certainly disappear. While wide-ranging wildlife like deer and turkey will do fine under these conditions, those with more particular needs, such as pine warblers and spruce grouse, will not. Less snowfall in winter also means fewer seasonal ponds and less breeding habitat for frogs, so spring evenings in Wisconsin may be quieter in the future.

Most of us came here by choice, and a full range of seasons was part of the draw. There's still time to mitigate these changes, but it will require an act of will and a real sense of place. This isn't so much an issue of politics as of geography. There will always be those who say not to worry, that the weather is always fickle, and—as for climate change—we'll just cross that bridge when we come to it.

Well, we've come to it.

MARCH

The Heart of Things

A RIVER SYSTEM is one of those vague territories, like a voting district, that we belong to without having to think about it very much. But I think about the Chippewa River at least a couple times a day. It heads in several lakes near the Michigan border, drains nearly ten thousand square miles of northern Wisconsin, then passes within two blocks of my house on its way to the Mississippi. Most mornings I walk to a red brick building on its bank to work. To get almost anywhere requires crossing the river, usually in traffic. In all of these passages, the river is a constant reference point, its height and color as much a measure of the day as the weather.

"How's the river today?" I'll ask without taking my eyes off the road. My wife or one of the kids will glance over the guardrail long enough to report that the river is looking high or low, murky with runoff or floating great panes of ice, its surface smooth as pressed steel or cut by a V-shaped wave whose tip is a retriever returning a stick to the man who threw it from shore. Somehow these things seem vital.

"To live by a large river is to be kept in the heart of things," the poet John Haines once wrote. The river he had in mind was the Tanana shortly after it emerges from the Alaska Range. I know this because I was a student of Haines at the University of Alaska and sometimes visited his homestead at Mile 68 on the Richardson Highway. From the squat little cabin I could look down on the Tanana in its glacial valley, braided channels in the wide gravel flats pulsing with snowmelt, all in the shadow of trackless mountains. Back then I imagined that keeping "in the heart of things"

34

would require isolation and a mythic landscape of snowcapped peaks and hanging glaciers. Now I think it just requires a river.

Counting railroad trestles, eight bridges span the Chippewa River within the city limits of my hometown. My favorite is the slim concrete footbridge connecting the campus where I work with the Fine Arts Center on the other side. I often stop at midspan, pedestrian and bicycle traffic flowing past, to look around. Downstream, the river curves around a sandstone bluff before sliding on toward the Mississippi; upstream is a second bridge filled with cars. But looking down into the water, straight down into the transparent panel of shade cast by the bridge, it's another world.

A river is what wildlife biologists call an "edge," a boundary where two habitats come together. From the footbridge, the transitional zone is most obvious where the willow, cottonwood, and phlox give way to a sand and cobble beach and the river itself. Two sets of lives meet in this narrow corridor—and not just aquatic and terrestrial. On a hot summer day, a flotilla of teenagers on inner tubes and air mattresses drifts slowly under the bridge, unaware they're sharing the Lower Chippewa with 112 species of fish, some no doubt looking up at the dark shapes blotting out the light. We habitually distinguish between our lives and those of animals—our reasoning/their instinct, our journey/their migration, our language/their silence. But a river blurs those differences. You wade deeper and deeper into the water until you're no longer walking upright on two limbs but doing the "crawl" on all fours and feeling strangely happy.

From the bridge I regularly see carp schooling nose to tail against the current and sometimes a soft-shelled turtle periscoping its long neck out of the water. The other river dwellers, the ones I can't see, usually leave tracks in the sand or fish bones, something to mark their passage.

For years, students have arranged the cobblestones on the beach into messages that can only be read, like a secret code, from the footbridge. The messages are clearly intended for those crossing the river. Sometimes I feel like I'm reading the personals section of the newspaper, others like I'm taking a test for color blindness. Is that a peace sign or a happy face? Sometimes, there are so many rock designs that the beach resembles an ancient petroform site, except the patterns last only until the next high water or until someone borrows the stones for a different message. Occasionally the rocks form an ongoing narrative.

Early one spring, "I LOVE YOU TERRY" appeared in stones on the upriver side of the bridge after the last snow melted. Next day, same spot, the rocks were reconfigured: "WILL YOU MARRY ME?" A March snowstorm later erased the message and the beach was a blank until a thaw revealed a single word outlined in pan ice: "YES."

Small Talk

MY FAVORITE BREAKFAST SPOT in Milwaukee was a café on Brady Street that doubled as a drugstore and movie house. The waitresses served eggs, sausage, and toast on thick crockery plates, then hovered around to make sure my coffee cup never dropped below half full. It was the perfect place to waste a morning. I was doing just that early one Saturday when a group of older men filed in and took a booth by the door, which I gathered was "their" table. Another man about the same age came through the door, and they all looked up. One of the men at the table pointed to the newcomer and said something. The newcomer threw back his hands in false alarm and said something back that made everyone laugh. My booth was too far for me to hear what was said, but the subject of conversation hardly mattered. They were just making small talk.

The role of small talk within the social contract never occurred to me until my first real job as a summer "intern" at an automobile assembly plant. My duties in the rear assembly division were to grab an axle dangling from a moving hook and insert it shaft-first into a housing sliding past on the assembly line, snap it in place with a quick hip thrust, then align the bolts so they could be tightened with a power wrench by the next person. The last two steps required a certain finesse that sometimes had me follow a misplaced shaft down the line, whacking at it rumba-style with my hip. I did this eight hours a day not including the half hour off for lunch and a fifteen-minute coffee break.

When the line shut down about midway through the shift, everyone retreated to the break table to shoot the breeze, play speed checkers, or just sit around smoking with a kind of religious intensity. Everyone but me. I'd spend my break time deep in a paperback novel, preparing myself for the greater world beyond the factory. After a while, my coworkers on the axle line began to merge with the characters in the novel I was reading until they were the same: rough men of every stripe who welcomed the earnest young protagonist they'd secretly nicknamed The Kid.

Then one day a coworker came over during break and suggested in a friendly way that The Kid pull his head out of his "book" (another word was used) and join the conversation. So I did.

I didn't know it then, but some people at the break table had risked their livelihoods for those fifteen minutes. Three years earlier, the UAW had gone on strike to force automakers to include a fifteen-minute paid break in the union contract. The Big Three eventually relented when they realized a coffee break was good for morale and that was good for productivity. We never talked about anything important during break; it was all small talk: brief, elliptical conversations that boomeranged around the table—the terrible heat from the blast furnace, our weekend plans, the eccentricities of the shop foreman. For fifteen minutes a day, we were all on the same page. Small talk kept the mind sharp even when the body was engaged in a numbingly repetitive job. It allowed people doing robot work to feel human.

Evolutionary psychologist Robin Dunbar argues that language developed among early humans not just to convey information—*Look, a saber-tooth tiger!*—but to solidify group cohesiveness. Primates accomplished this social function through grooming, but as larger groups made grooming impractical, language evolved to take its place. Gossip is the equivalent of primate grooming;

it's nit-picking, and even the highly educated benefit from it. Monitoring talk at a British university refectory, Dunbar found that "social relationships and personal experiences accounted for about 70 per cent of conversation time."

That was certainly the case when I first started teaching. There wasn't much difference between the factory break table and English Department coffee room except perhaps syntax. Every morning professors dropped in for a jolt of caffeine before class, a little jawboning with colleagues, some good-natured teasing. "Speaking of the fool in Elizabethan drama . . . ," Professor Brown might say as a late arrival walked through the door. The teasing wasn't mean-spirited; it was a sign of acceptance. Nearly all the faculty, mostly male then, had been drafted into the military or had some other prior experience in jobs where they were paid to do something other than talk, so talk became a freebie, a way to kill time, a form of amusement.

Now that the older generation has retired, the coffee room is empty. The automatic drip machine with its twelve-cup carafe has been replaced by a device that makes one lonely cup at a time. "That way," a colleague explained, "there's no waste."

There's also no small talk. Faculty microwave their lunch in the coffee room and then rush back to their offices to eat alone. Laughter, on the rare occasions one hears it, is likely to come from the main office on days the Central Stores guy delivers a pallet of duplicating paper. Instead of heading off to the next delivery, he'll stop to joke with the secretaries. One of the women jokes back, and pretty soon they're all laughing. The laughter swells and builds until it spills into the hallway and causes Professor So-and-so to look up from his computer screen and wonder: How can people with no formal training in language have such fun using it?

So here's a generational puzzle: Who killed the Coffee Czar? The new faculty are every bit as friendly as their predecessors, so why, when you joke with them, do they act as if invited on a snipe hunt? Why can't they make small talk?

It's no coincidence that the coffee room's decline began about the time the university was wired to the Internet. Communications that once required a face-to-face encounter now occur electronically. Birthday greetings, condolences, good news and bad—they're sent and received alone. My Facebook friends share pictures of their children along with the seafood dinner they've just ordered; they share thoughts and musings about almost everything in stream-of-consciousness postings, but I can't say we've actually had a conversation. When someone forwards an online joke—a dig at sexism or a book banning or some other nonstarter—the target is a million miles away, not in the next office. What's lost in the Facebook era is the give-and-take of conversation, the sometime risky choice of words that depends so much on reading the other person's face.

On the early frontier, a fur trader approaching an unfamiliar village or encampment would discharge his musket into the air. The shot served two purposes. It announced the stranger's arrival, and, more importantly, it demonstrated that the musket was now unloaded, a gesture that was literally "disarming." Small talk works the same way. The opening salvo may be a joke or some other pointless comment, but the message is always the same: I come in peace.

Leopold's Journal

ON THE SECOND FLOOR of the Forest and Wildlife Ecology building on the University of Wisconsin campus is a glass case that holds a few iconographic objects that belonged to the department's founder: typewritten manuscripts, unfilled archery tags, some hand-built long bows, and a well-oiled Winchester .30-30. The carbine dates from 1909, when a young Aldo Leopold, fresh from Yale, carried it in a saddle scabbard as horseback-riding ranger with the US Forest Service in Arizona. It's the same rifle, according to his biographer, that Leopold used to dispatch a she-wolf in "Thinking Like a Mountain." Perhaps the best-known essay in *A Sand County Almanac,* it recounts how the author, "full of trigger-itch," reflexively gunned down the wolf as she forded a river with her pups and then watched "the fierce green light dying in her eyes."

Thirty years after the event, Leopold had to be goaded into writing the scene by a former graduate student who suggested the professor's writing was, well, too professorial. Instead of simply presenting conclusions, the former student encouraged Leopold to show the evolution in his thinking about Nature, the soul-searching as well as facts that led to the conclusions—and to do that he'd have to admit his own mistakes. The resulting narrative describes an almost a Saul-like conversion in the desert.

> *I thought that because fewer wolves meant more deer, that no wolves would mean a hunter's paradise. But after seeing the green fire die, I sensed that neither the wolf nor the mountain agreed with such a view.*

I'd stopped by the department to interview one of the faculty on deer-wolf relationships when he offered to show me the glass case tucked unobtrusively away in a committee room. For me, it was like visiting a church and seeing the reliquary of its patron saint. Aldo Leopold created the first school of game management in the country at Madison and was instrumental in moving wildlife decisions away from politicians and into the hands of professional biologists, who could be expected to take the long view. The state legislature has recently wrested it back by legalizing the first wolf hunt in half a century. Leopold could be as rhapsodic as any nature writer, but he was a scientist first and put facts above emotions. The subjects he addressed in the 1930s and '40s—the role of predators, the idea of land as something more than an economic commodity—are thorny matters we're still arguing today.

An hour's drive north of Madison lies the "Shack," the weekend retreat Leopold and his family built along the Wisconsin River. The only difference between the black-and-white pictures of the Shack taken seventy years ago and now is the deep pool of shade from the pines the family planted along the river. The 12½ by 18 chicken coop was the only structure standing when Leopold bought the eighty-acre abandoned farm in 1935. After mucking out the chicken droppings, the Leopolds added a shed-roofed bunkhouse, fireplace and chimney, wooden floor, and battens to the Shack's upright board siding. Still, you wonder how a family of seven managed to squeeze inside at the end of the day. An optimist, Leopold took the long view that land reduced to "corn stubble, cockleburs and broken fences" could eventually be restored to health. "On this sand farm in Wisconsin, first worn out and then abandoned by our bigger-and-better society, we try to rebuild, with shovel and axe, what we are losing elsewhere."

I first read *A Sand County Almanac* during the interminable darkness of an Alaskan winter. Like a lot of people who'd fled to the Far North in their twenties, I had a cynic's view of anything short of untrammeled wilderness. What a surprise then to be caught up in a book about a landscape that had been thoroughly trammeled. Leopold had arranged the first part of the book around a calendar year at the Shack to tie together scattered pieces written over a long stretch of time. There were ecological lessons embedded in each sketch but so artfully that I hardly noticed. The book read like a Midwestern version of *A Swiss Family Robinson*: a resourceful father leading his family as they build a shelter out of salvaged materials, plant trees and wildflowers, count waves of migrating waterfowl. *A Sand County Almanac* switched lenses for me. Instead of viewing nature through a telescope trained on distant mountains, Leopold used a magnifying glass to examine ordinary wonders: robins and jewelweed and sandbars in a wide river—all the things I'd left behind. The book made me homesick.

The genesis of most of the essays in *A Sand County Almanac* can be found in the extensive journals and diaries Leopold kept throughout his life. Rising before dawn, he would sit on a bench outside the Shack with binoculars and wristwatch to record the order of birdsong. He made field notes in a small address book kept in his shirt pocket and at the end of the day would enter these observations in a leather-bound journal. The entries are methodically organized by topic: weather, phenology, mammals, birds, and work done on the Shack.

The entry for March 23–24, 1940—"clear, very cold (nearly zero)"—suggests a dispassionate observer who seems to notice everything:

> *Mammals—Many deer tracks all over place. Deer have been browsing poison ivy at some time during the winter. Red squirrels active at woodpile. Saw 6 rabbits in 4 hours. Rabbits have been budding the elm limbs we left on the ice—also a little barking but they don't like bark much. Found a deer mouse nest in the icebox containing 1 live mouse and one dead one, obviously frozen. Nest built of lint pulled off the bedding.*

It's probably inevitable to compare Leopold with America's other great self-marooned journal writer, Henry David Thoreau. Both men framed their writing in a specific place, not wilderness but a spot close to home. H.D. Thoreau was twenty-eight when he moved down the road from Concord to Walden Pond; Leopold acquired his "sand farm" later in life, a middle-aged man in the grip of obligations—familial and professional. As a fulltime professor, Leopold sat on countless civic and university boards, and while Thoreau spent a night in jail, he never had to endure the blather of a committee meeting. Thoreau logged more than two million words in his diaries, material he later mined for books, and the diaries, like the books, are a flood of ideas soliloquized in an exuberant first person. Leopold's journals are less literary and less personal, more an inventory of things—animal tracks and plant blooms and weather—that could later be abstracted into ideas. His phenological records are so precise and extensive they've been used to track changes in species brought about by climate change. On those occasions he wrote about people, the pronoun he used most often wasn't "I" but "we."

Thoreau's last words as he lay dying of tuberculosis at his family's home in Concord were "Indian" and "moose." Nobody knows what Leopold may have said before he suffered a fatal heart attack fighting a grass fire near the Shack on April 21, 1948. He'd made the usual field notes in his pocket notebook that morning. After the fire, the notebook was found on Leopold's body, its edges charred from the flames, but the neat, almost slantless handwriting still legible. The final entry is "Lilac shoots 2" long."

Maps

A FEW MONTHS AGO I rented a car equipped with an electronic navigation system to drive across Illinois, a state so flat and open that getting lost there requires an act of will. Along with the dash-mounted screen, a computerized voice narrated my trip as a series of turns. It was a woman's voice, professionally reassuring, suggesting with great tact that I "turn left in one-quarter mile" or "get in the right lane." Whenever I altered the route, for instance by turning off I-39 for gas, the voice chanted: "As soon as possible, make a legal U-turn" until I returned to the interstate. The voice was never wrong and it never lost patience or developed the cool edge my wife's voice sometimes gets when I navigate by the seat of my pants. It was an omniscient narrator, like having God as my copilot. On the drive home, I switched it off.

Given the option, I'll take a paper map over an electronic navigation system anytime—unless I'm circumnavigating the globe or traversing the Alps—because following a GPS amounts to tunnel vision. It informs the traveler only what's directly in front of him, not what's off to the side or where he's been or might want to go in the future.

In early spring when other people pore over seed catalogues, I read maps with the same sense of anticipation. Maps abstract places into pieces of information, like elevation and vegetation, that allow one to see the bigger picture. They're also pretty. I have file cabinet drawers crammed with maps in accordion folds and cardboard tubes: plat maps, USGS quadrant maps, road maps, navigational charts for the Upper Mississippi River, inserts from

National Geographic, maps of national parks and forests, county maps, city maps, a satellite image of the Arctic Coast of Alaska, a hiking map of Wales. The collection represents past trips and those in the planning stages as well as places I'll never go or that, in a few cases, no longer exist.

Hanging from a wall in my office is a large topographical map of Buffalo County, issued by the Wisconsin Geological Survey, E. F. Bean, state geologist, presiding. It's a beautiful chart with azure creeks and rivers and deep umber contour lines so convoluted with the elevation extremes between bluff tops and coulees that it looks like a slice of Switzerland. The Mississippi River, which forms the county's western border, frays into side channels and backwater sloughs, and beyond the river, where Minnesota should be, is an expanse of white space that might as well be labeled *terra incognita*. The map offers a one-dimensional view of the landscape, although from a canoe that's just the way things look: a long, linear shoreline broken by an archipelago of jungle-y islands. It was drawn in 1932, a few years before the Army Corps of Engineers constructed a series of locks and dams to provide a navigation channel and thwart the free-flowing Mississippi's inclination to flood, so many of the sloughs have since disappeared beneath the dams' backwaters. And it's not just the river that's changed. The map shows each valley as a kind of separate kingdom: Norwegian Valley, Irish Valley, Upper Irish Valley, Jahn's Valley, Montana Ridge, Trout Creek, Little Bluebell, Pine Creek Bluff. Most of the valleys have their own rural school (a black square with a flag on top) as well as church (a black square with a cross on top). It's a world that's absolutely vanished except on this map.

Once, flying in a Cessna two-seater to a Gwich'in Indian village on the south flank of the Brooks Range in Alaska, I asked the bush pilot if the low peaks sailing below us were part of the White Mountains.

"Beats me," he shrugged over the engine's roar. The bush pilot explained that he'd set the coordinates for the village into the plane's GPS before takeoff and it gave him an unerring compass heading to follow, so he didn't need to know where he was at any given moment. Then he resumed his loose-limbed posture of professional boredom.

I wasn't bored in the least. I spread a 1:24,000-scale topographical map across my knees and confirmed that the peaks were, in fact, the White Mountains. Now I was busy making contingency plans just in case the plane developed engine problems or ran out of gas or the pilot succumbed to food poisoning. In that case, knowing where I was at the moment would be as important as knowing where I intended to go. Presuming I survived the crash, I'd build a raft and float down Birch Creek to the village of the same name, carefully lining my flimsy craft through many rapids conveniently indicated by slash marks on the map.

Walleye

ONE NIGHT when the ice has gone out but the air still feels sharply of winter, I'll walk down the road from my favorite North Woods tavern and shine a flashlight into a narrow stream. If my timing is right, the beam will be fragmented into luminous points of greenish light, so many that I'll feel as if I'm staring up at constellations instead of leaning over a bridge. The light is reflected off the *tapetum lucidum,* the iridescent layer of pigment surrounding the pupils of walleyes come up from the deep recesses of the lake to spawn in the shallows of the feeder stream. It's difficult to convey the strangeness of the scene: dozens of spawning walleye, all male, churning and roiling the water around a female twice their size. On the few occasions when a group of us drifted down from the tavern, nobody spoke above a whisper. The silence wasn't just from witnessing a sex act performed with the dispassion of machinery; it was a reaction to seeing a secret part of the lake suddenly made public.

Back at the tavern, we'll sit beneath a row of antlered heads arranged above the bar as if they were party to the conversation. Lots of things are said in a night's drinking. Sometimes an offhand remark opens the door on a private life you'd just as soon remain dark, but once open there's no shutting that door. The deer heads withhold judgment.

Twenty years ago, the talk in every North Woods tavern was of Indians spearing walleyes. The Chippewa had retained their right to fish in this way because a forward-thinking chief named *Aish-*

49

ke-gi-bosh, or Flat Mouth, refused to sign a treaty in 1837 ceding the northern third of Wisconsin to the United States unless it guaranteed the tribe's right to fish, hunt, and gather wild food in the ceded territory. Federal courts had repeatedly verified these rights, but for a time in the late 1980s antitreaty protests became an annual rite of spring.

On one such night, I followed a squad car's flashing blue lights north on Highway 51 to Trout Lake, where a crowd had assembled at a boat landing to protest Chippewa spearing. The people streaming from their cars toward the landing might have been mistaken for fans headed to a Friday night football game—the bowl of klieg lights, the unseasonable cold, the rising cheers—until you got closer and heard the racial slurs and saw the placards: "Save a Walleye, Spear an Indian." A snow fence and police in riot gear separated a small circle of Indians beating on a kettle-sized drum from a crowd of white protesters dressed in blaze orange hunting clothes. And there were cheerleaders, grown men bellowing out the sort of ugliness some of their neighbors might have secretly harbored but never voiced outside of a tavern.

Out on the dark lake, Chippewa spearers searched for spawning walleye in the shallows. The beams of their headlamps made them visible from the shore.

"It's hard enough to take the name-calling," a Lac du Flambeau spearer told me afterwards, "but it's worse thinking someone might kill you. I've been hit with rocks and ball-bearings fired from slingshots. We're not doing this to be cocky. We're doing it for our kids because if we don't stand up for our rights, they're not going to have anything when they get older."

The future he was imagining that night twenty years ago is now the present. I suppose there is much to be grateful for on this unmarked anniversary. Walleye still spawn on cold spring evenings even as the Chippewa take their portion. Nobody got killed, and the protests eventually petered out. We've all settled into being good neighbors now. It's almost as if none of this ever happened.

But sometimes I'll see a light out in the darkness and remember those long-ago spring nights and wonder if anyone else remembers. How could people forget what was said at the boat landings and made public? How could they forget their own silence?

APRIL

Driving North

DRIVING NORTH IN APRIL, I don't look for signs of spring so much as guarantees. Of course, the farther north I travel, the more the road circles back to winter or at least mid-March. The view out the windshield is like time-lapse photography run backwards: trillium cease blooming a few miles north of Highway 29, poplar leaves fold back into reddish buds, and even the shifting sky seems to have lost warmth. New growth, where it's managed to push out of the soil, is pointillistic and more brilliantly green for being surrounded by grays and browns. It's an Easter week landscape— death and resurrection all jumbled together.

The trip itself is one sure sign of spring since I make it each year regardless of weather. To keep the two-hour drive interesting, I take one route going up and another driving back. The route up passes through one of the most rural, least-peopled areas in the state. Small towns get smaller, all but the evangelical radio stations fade into static, and not a single traffic light to slow me down. The land is unrelentingly flat and poorly drained, a mix of farms and woods. It isn't vacationland, in other words, unless your idea of a vacation is milking cows or cutting pulpwood. With the snow gone, what's revealed in spring is the land's pure geometry: perfect rectangles of muddy pasture or tilled brown fields that abruptly end where a vertical wall of poplar begins. There's a stark beauty to all this empty space carved out of woods and bare earth and held in place by a few fence lines.

The solitary houses along the way stick out in their isolation: a nicely dormered farmhouse where I stopped one summer to buy clover honey, a newly built Amish house with work horses and a privy, a squat trailer on the edge of an alder swamp. I've followed the trailer's fortunes over the years as outbuildings have been added and ownership changed. The newest resident has bolted a small satellite dish to the roof to better connect himself to the world.

What would it be like to live here?

That question has been my version of a car-ride game ever since I started riding in cars. The game reached its pitch when I was traveling around the country in my twenties and imagined each new place as a potential home. Like a lot of people back then, I carried a well-worn copy of *Walden* in my backpack with passages underlined that confirmed things I already believed. One of those passages was, "Wherever I sat, there I might live, and the landscape radiated from me accordingly."

At the time I thought Thoreau meant that every destination came with an entirely different scenario attached to it, a whole other life, and the great challenge was choosing the right place. Live in a city and become one thing, move to the country and become something else.

Now I'm not so sure. One advantage of getting older is that you know how things turned out; you didn't end up in that fishing village on the coast or the mountain hamlet and never will. Did you miss out entirely on that other life? Who knows? Place matters but probably less than other externals like family or friends or work. That's because the space we carve out for our lives is more about time than geography, and since most lives follow a similar trajectory, it's reasonable to assume you can be happy (or not) anywhere.

Not long after getting married, I moved into a trailer like the one along this road, a tear-shaped affair attached to a one-room house in the middle of a pine-bordered field. It was our first home. It was also cramped and impossible to heat. I didn't expect to stay there forever, but while I did it seemed like the epicenter of the world, and each morning when I stepped out the door "the landscape radiated from me accordingly."

So that's what I imagine the fellow in this trailer thinks as he steps into the pale spring sunlight to survey his alder swamp, sees out of the corner of his eye a car speeding north, and wonders, if only for a moment, where it might be going.

Crane Count

ONE APRIL MORNING before daybreak, I stood alongside a marsh looking for sandhill cranes or, at least, hoping to hear them. The marsh was bordered by tag alder and dogwood and neatly split by a gravel road where an ornithologist, her husband, and I waited. We stood in the dark drinking coffee from a thermos and taking some comfort in the notion that we weren't alone. This was the morning of the Annual Midwest Crane Count, and hundreds of volunteers were standing in marshes all over Wisconsin.

The clangor of cranes traditionally ushers in the spring, signaling the farmer to plant his seeds. But the temperature in our marsh this morning was in the low twenties and patches of snow remained among the brown reeds. Karen Voss, the ornithologist, worried that the cold weather had delayed the crane's northward migration. The Great Lakes population of greater sandhill cranes winters in the pine flats and prairies of Florida, feeding on sorghum and winter wheat and the occasional frog. By late February the cranes fly north with the lengthening days, corkscrewing into the sky in a great, whirling axis reaching altitudes as high as thirteen thousand feet. After a stopover in northern Indiana, the cranes regroup and head for nesting grounds in the Upper Midwest. The annual count was scheduled to occur just after the crane's presumed arrival and before the secretive business of incubating eggs, a period when sandhills should be their most visible, trumpeting and dancing as pairs choose and defend nesting territories.

All I'd heard that morning was the distant wash of trucks on the interstate to the east. But the sky was starting to lighten. The road and woods took shape in the silvery half-light. Sunrise is the cue, the reason the cock crows—and apparently every other bird. Voss proceeded to pick individual singers out of the cacophony: the *huhuhu*-ing of snipe, the *beezp-beezp*-ing of woodcock, the gurgle of red-winged blackbirds, the flywheel drumming of a ruffed grouse in the bordering woods. But no trumpeting cranes.

Snow began to fall, a heavy, wet snow that stuck to alder branches and abruptly put a lid on the birdsong.

"I've spent so many mornings like this," Voss sighed, "standing in a marsh, dressed to the teeth, just waiting."

As she spoke, an enormous bird glided across the marsh, a flying cruciform whose long wings moved effortlessly against the falling snow. We all trained our binoculars to intersect its flight. It was a heron.

The great blue heron fairly parachuted into the marsh and alighted on the lip of a beaver dam. Magnified by my binocular lenses, the heron appeared to scowl, sensing perhaps a reception intended for someone else.

When settlers first came to Wisconsin, cranes were abundant, especially in the central sand counties, but in 1929 when Aldo Leopold surveyed sandhill nesting grounds in the state he found only five breeding pairs. As cranes were shot for their meat and marshes ditched and drained for farmland, the sandhill seemed destined for the same fate as the nearly extinct whooping crane. Writing in *A Sand County Almanac*, Leopold imagined a bleak and imminent future in which "the last crane will trumpet his farewell and spiral from the great marsh." Fortunately, he was wrong. A ban on hunting and the establishment of state and federal wildlife refuges brought the sandhills back from the brink of extirpation to a current estimated seventy-two thousand in Wisconsin—so many, in fact, that some legislators have proposed opening a new hunting season on cranes.

Hunting would not be the biggest threat to sandhill cranes. In the past two centuries, about half the state's wetlands have been lost, so while sandhill numbers are up, there's less suitable habitat for them. Of course, it's easier to elicit interest in a large iconic creature like a sandhill crane than an unglamorous habitat like wetlands even though the wetlands clearly need saving. Hence the crane count. On a designated morning in April hundreds of people who wouldn't otherwise venture into a swamp do so to tally sandhill cranes.

"I don't know anybody who sees a crane and doesn't feel moved by it," said Voss. "There's something to labeling things. If you see an animal and know its name, you feel a claim to it, a proprietary interest."

Later that week Voss and I drove to a state wildlife area in the eastern part of the county, a checkerboard of jack pine, aspen, and diked marshes. The sun was up, shining through the trees, and the day was growing warm, almost springlike. We followed a dike across open water filled with teal and ring-necked ducks when a sandhill crane suddenly broke from the willows and filled the marsh with air horn blasts as if we'd stumbled over a trip wire.

GA-ROOO . . . GA-ROOO-AAA . . . GA-ROOO-AAA!

The klaxon bugling was a guard call, meant to alert other cranes. The sheer volume and reverberation were the result of the crane's remarkable windpipe, nearly five feet long and coiled like a French horn in the keel of the breastbone. Cupping its long wings, the spooked crane touched down on the far dike. Aware it was being watched, the crane ambled across the dike in a long-gaited, professorial stride, implied lecture notes held behind its back.

The crane we'd been watching stepped off the dike and momentarily disappeared. Suddenly there were two cranes standing on either side of a reedy, oval mound. They began to bugle in unison, a kind of duet. The crane we'd been following, then, was a male, and the unison call announced that he was ready to share nesting duties. (Cranes make admirable spouses, mating for life and splitting domestic chores such as incubating eggs.) The male bird pointed his beak skyward, arching his long neck and trumpeting one sustained note. The female arched her neck, flipping her beak up twice and bugling two notes that bracketed his one, so the songs blended together.

Free now to feed and preen, the female crane wandered along the dike, occasionally stopping to dabble her beak in the mud and smooth her feathers. She was applying makeup. The ferric oxide in the muck turned her gray wings a rusty brown. Then in two hops she was airborne, snake-neck extended, stilt-legs trailing, winging up into a china-blue sky.

Camouflage

WHY DO VISITORS to the state capital feel compelled to walk down State Street in a pair of Mossy Oak jeans and a four-toned woodland pattern shirt with matching cap? It's certainly not to blend into the urban scene. On the contrary, it's a willful attempt to stick out. Wearing camouflage clothing in the city is a flag of choice, like wearing one's high school colors to the state basketball championship. It's a fashion statement, and what it says is "I'm not from around here but someplace else, a place whose main street isn't lined with head shops and fusion restaurants." Sometimes there's a small-minded complacency to all this, a fear that failing to dress for dinner like you just stepped out of a duck blind might lead to ordering escargot and jesting with the waiters in French.

Unsurprisingly, the French invented the modern art of camouflage, a word that derives from *camoufler*, "to disguise." At the beginning of the First World War, the French military discovered that the snappy white gloves and red pantaloons worn by their troops made for easy targets in the trenches, so they established a Section de Camouflage and staffed it with Impressionist and Cubist painters, sculptors, and other artistic types. These *camoufleurs* designed artificial trees to disguise artillery as well uniforms like the "horizon blue" jacket that allowed the wearer to blend into the landscape.

My own camouflage ensemble is a ragtag mixture of army surplus and commercial gear. The jacket, pants, and hat use the blotchy, four-colored woodland pattern recently discontinued by our military, while my facemask, gloves, and game bag are the latest photorealistic Mossy Oak pattern. Since the scene I'm trying to blend into is a wooded coulee bottom, I'm usually too green or too brown depending on which five-day period I draw for spring turkey hunting.

After blowing my owl hooter—*Whooo cooks for you-ooo?*—to locate roosting turkeys, I'll set up by flashlight on the edge of an oak opening. I'll pose two rubber decoys (Mr. Tom and Ms. Hen) as provocatively as possible at the end of shooting lane I've brushed out of the woods. Then I'll lean against a tree to break up my silhouette, cover my outstretched legs with dry leaves and ferns, and wait for sunrise. If I lie perfectly still, chickadees sometimes alight on my shoulders. And once a yearling doe tiptoed within a few feet, sniffing and stamping the ground, uncertain of what she was dealing with until I stirred like a corpse in a haunted house and frightened her away.

Lying on the ground like this, covered with dry leaves and bits of fern, I feel like the Green Man. I first saw the Green Man in England, carved into one of the fourteenth-century stone arches in Lincoln Cathedral—a human face peering out from behind a mask of oak leaves. If someone hadn't pointed him out, I wouldn't have noticed the face in the leaves. He's the original *camoufleur*. Writing on the Green Man's persistence, John Fowles observed that "the myth is so profound and universal because it is constantly 'played' inside every individual consciousness." Maybe what Fowles means is that the image of man in nature (or vice versa) is a reminder of our common share in the cycle of life. Birth and death and rebirth. At any rate, that's what I think about when I lie against the earth again after a long winter's dormancy and smell the mix of leaf rot and new growth, life pushing out of decay. Somehow I'm a part of this.

Let's not forget the shotgun on my knee. I'm here to take advantage of nature's impulse to recreate itself, namely the polygamous bent of male turkeys in the spring to mate with every hen possible. As the sun rises and birdsong begins in earnest, I chime in as the disembodied voice of a lonesome hen. It's a deeper deception than wearing camouflage and one that ends, I hope, with a bang.

When I was young and polygamous, I'd sometimes drive girlfriends into the country and park beside a turkey farm where a thousand white gobblers were counting the days until Thanksgiving. Rolling down the car window, I'd yell "Gobble, gobble, gobble!!" and a thousand turkeys would gobble back in a roaring, surflike echo. Then I'd fold my arms and wobble my chin like Mussolini on a balcony. After one performance a girlfriend coolly observed that at least one turkey was on the wrong side of the fence.

Domestic turkeys are, of course, notoriously stupid. Their wild cousins, however, are wary and discerning and protective of the flock. Equipped with telescopic eyesight and a 270-degree field of vision, a wild turkey can detect the blink of the eye at one hundred yards and locate sounds as far as a mile away. Set against these natural defenses is the turkey's romantic heart.

My calling has advanced since the days when I yodeled out car windows. Now I use a box call to yip, putt, and cluck. Then, if a tom gobbles in response, I finish off with the cutting call of an "excited hen"—a series of short, rising yelps that end on a plaintive note of inquiry. With any luck, Mr. Tom will fix on my siren song and come a-running. His gobbling will grow louder and more urgent as he shortens the distance between us, and—if he's not distracted by a real hen along the way—he'll break out of the tree line and into the clearing to confront my decoy couple, Ms. Hen and his rubbery rival. Then, throwing caution to the wind, he'll unfurl his great, coppery tail feathers behind him like a cape and begin to strut—another fool for love.

Green Acres

SOMETIMES WHEN I'm at the cabin, instead of hearing a barred owl or grouse or loon or some other North Woods sound, I'll hear a Holstein cow bellowing from the dairy farm down the road. It's a deep-throated foghorn of a call, conveying who knows what—desire, loneliness, milking time? There's a bovine urgency to the bellowing, an insistence that while cows might seem out of place in northern Wisconsin, they aren't—or weren't.

The epoch of small-scale agriculture that followed lumbering in northern Wisconsin lasted a few generations before giving way to the era of summer cottagers, although a few old-timers can still point out stands of pine that were formerly pasture or tillable fields. My neighbor on the Elk River remembers when a farmer used to drive his cows across an iron trestle bridge so they could graze on the scrub grass and weeds where my cabin now stands. Farming was a hardscrabble life during the Great Depression and especially in the Cutover. After the stumps were pulled and burned, there was endless rock to pick, and even then the soil was often full of clay and poorly drained. Most of the immigrant families who gambled on this grand experiment at the turn of the last century threw in the towel during the 1930s and let their fields revert to forest. The few working farms that remain belong to the grandchildren of the stubborn few who didn't.

So it's surprising to witness an agricultural resurgence in the North Woods, not so much of crops or livestock but the iconography of farming: hay bales lined up beside a realtor's sign, a solitary calf staked like a puppy in a neighbor's front yard. These symbols are intended for an audience of one: the township tax assessor.

In 1995 the state legislature passed a law that changed the basis for assessing farmland from one based on market value to one based on the land's agricultural use. The intent was to stem the steady loss of cropland in Wisconsin, approximately thirty thousand acres a year. But in effect the law often made farmland more attractive to developers, who could hold and even subdivide the land at miniscule tax rates as long as they could show an agricultural "use." For instance, the waterfront parcels upriver of my place sell for $10,000 an acre but are assessed at only $127 an acre because the landowner hired a real farmer to bale hay on the property, so it qualifies as "third grade tillable." The difference in the township's tax revenue is made up by those who don't pretend to farm.

"When I first started assessment work," my friend Bob Elkins said, "the most common phrase I heard was 'I just want to pay my fair share.' But lately I've been receiving out-of-state phone calls that sound like this: 'I'm looking for a large tract of land and I want to make sure this land is not being taxed at full value.'"

Neighboring states like Minnesota, which are also trying to protect agricultural land, have tax laws that require individuals to prove they've earned income from farming the land as opposed to setting out symbols. My father-in-law spent a lifetime farming and it took a physical toll on him, though he never complained because he loved working the land. He hated movies and TV shows that made farm life seem simpleminded and carefree, a refuge from big city realities.

So I've come up with a means test for those who would take tax breaks meant for real farmers. Under my plan, the tax assessor would assume the role of Troll-at-the-Gate and assign each applicant seven tasks. Anyone who's spent time on a farm can devise his or her own list of representative chores. Here's mine:

1. Take out a banknote this spring to test your clairvoyance on summer precipitation and fall commodity prices.
2. Run a three-hundred-pound bull calf into a squeeze chute after separating him from his outraged mother. Reach in with both hands and revise calf's gender.
3. Walk behind a stone boat and pick rock all day.
4. A bearing's gone out on your combine in midfield. Get out the wrenches.
5. Wait at the grain elevator with other farmers while your corn is weighed. Make ironic jokes at your own expense— e.g., the banknote.
6. Inform the party in hot-orange hats that hunting rights to your back forty are worth more than the bottle of schnapps they've offered.
7. Scrape the cow yard and spread the manure on winter fields before they thaw. When the spreader gets snarled with a piece of baling wire, reach in and carefully remove it. Very carefully.

Petitioners who successfully complete all seven tasks may in good conscience take the agricultural discount on their property taxes. Those who fail are condemned to pick rock.

MAY

Lilacs

BELOW THE LAST DAM, the Chippewa River becomes the sum of all its northern tributaries: a broad, slow-moving river flowing through farmland and prairie remnants. A few miles downstream of Caryville, part of the river makes a sudden left turn—enough to float a canoe between wooded islands. The tangled banks close in and the sky narrows to a slot of blue. At that point, the side channel seems less a split in a big river than a separate river altogether—smaller and more intimate, the water braided in places around sand and cobble bars like a Western trout stream.

Lining the canoe through the shallows one morning, fishing rod in hand, I looked up to see a cloud of purple blossoms hovering over the cutbank. The first wildflowers were out—phlox and bluebells—but this great red-violet arc overshadowed all of them. It was a lilac bush, tall as a tree; its flower clusters drooping twenty feet in the air were heavy with perfume. Against the canopy of river birch and silver maple, the domestic lilac looked as out of place as a racehorse among a herd of zebra. How did it get here? Bushwhacking through tall grass, I found the answer: a ruined silo and a cellar full of brambles. So the lilac had once shaded a now-vanished farmhouse. Until 1900 a farming community had thrived on the island, connected to the mainland by bridge and ferry. Three hundred people lived in the settlement with their own church, schoolhouse, post office, store, and shingle mill. Now there was nothing but jack pine and brambles and this one genteel survivor. Sometimes, bird hunting up north, I've stumbled across a solitary apple tree stranded in a field or an old pasture gone to aspen. But it was always a volunteer, planted with no more intention than a cow pausing to relieve herself. This was different. Someone had brought the lilac as rootstock to the island and planted it precisely here between farmhouse and river.

"A woman," my wife corrected me the next day. "A woman would have planted it."

She was thinking of her own family farm. Around the turn of the last century her grandmother had planted peonies and other perennials in a floral border around the family's farmhouse. For the grandmother, a generation removed from pioneers, flowers symbolized a degree of mastery over nature. They announced that the residents of the farmhouse no longer scratched out a living on the land but could afford to cultivate plants not intended as food for humans or livestock, plants whose only purpose was beauty. Almost a century later, before the local fire department burned down the old farmhouse in a training exercise, my wife rescued the peonies and transplanted them to our backyard, where every summer their white puffs recall the long-ago grandmother.

Similarly, I try to imagine the woman who planted the lilac, a Laurey or Aunt Eller, gazing out her front window at the lavender blossoms, knowing they'd last only until the next rainstorm beat them from the bush. She would have taken a paring knife to fill a few vases with blossoms, enough so the entire farmhouse smelled like her dressing table for at least a week.

One year after spring floods swept away the bridge, the people abandoned the island and the shingle mill and moved to a village downriver. Their farms gradually reverted to bottomland forest and prairie, except for the lilac, which has thrived without our presence. The lilac has its own intentions, mainly to reach sunlight, which explains its great height. You'd need an extension ladder now to gather the blossoms, though they're not beyond the reach of butterflies and bees and other pollinators. Although we like to think it's the reverse, plants use us no less than they use other creatures to survive and propagate. The color and scent of the blossoms still attract butterflies even as they once attracted a woman to plant a lilac between her front door and the river for what she imagined were her own intentions.

Night Shift

SOME NIGHTS AFTER SUPPER I'll walk out on the cabin deck and smoke a cigar. The fragrant smoke keeps the bugs away, except for moths attracted to the motion light above the door. Once that light shuts off, it's like a curtain being drawn or maybe another one going up. The river becomes the whooshing sound of itself, and the thousand spring peepers in the swamp behind the cabin blend into a single monstrous trilling. I'll sit on a deck chair listening to the flutter of moth wings and wonder what else is out there in the dark.

Judging from tracks along the river, animals work the night shift around here. Every summer a snapping turtle hauls herself from the water and digs a hole along the shoulder of the road to lay her eggs. Then a night or so later a skunk digs the eggs out and eats them. All this happens under cover of darkness, so when I walk along the road the next morning and connect the two events—the loose dirt and flattened eggshells—into a narrative, it's a little shocking; it's like reading in the morning paper that the people next door were in an accident. Who knew?

I'm thinking of last spring, when I crossed the bridge by the cabin and saw a family of skunks along the side of the road. Skunks are such nocturnal animals that the sight of them—mother and seven kits—parading in front of their den at high noon seemed an anomaly even though they must have been living in that den, unseen, for months. Black eyed and button nosed, the kits alternately nuzzled mom to feed or practiced waddling single file behind her. They looked clownish and sweet and no trouble at all.

For the next couple days I'd find every excuse to walk across the bridge and watch the skunk show—little Pepe Le Pews minus the straw boaters and canes. They seemed oblivious to the traffic or the fact that visibility put them at risk. Their mother had chosen the den site while there was snow on the ground, and she would soon lead the kits to another location—perhaps under my deck. Meanwhile, I'd heard grumbling on our side of the bridge. It was only a matter of time, neighbors said, until the clowning stopped and the skunks reverted to their true selves as nature's stink bombs. There was talk of a preemptive strike.

Years ago my wife live-trapped an animal that had been raiding her vegetable garden. It turned out to be a skunk. The animal control people couldn't send anyone to dispatch the skunk until after the weekend, so for three days she fed the captive skunk cantaloupe and squash from the garden and waited for it to revert to type. When it didn't, she threw a blanket over the trap, loaded it into the trunk of her car, drove out in the country, and let the skunk go.

I'd never have done that because I worry too much about eventualities—foreseeing trouble before it happens. Anyway, we were living in the country now, and the skunks had crossed a line by showing themselves. I resolved to deal with this moral quandary in the usual way, which is to say I did nothing.

The next day a car sat parked by the bridge long enough that my wife asked me to investigate. I didn't recognize the red-faced man, but whatever he was doing he felt confident enough to do in broad daylight. As soon as he put a plastic bucket in the back of his car and sped away, I knew what he'd been up to. He had dealt with eventualities by drowning them in the den.

Some nights I'll sit outside and let the big Polyphemus moths powder my nose with their feathery wings. Other times I get a strange notion to leave the deck and wander in the dark. But it would mean leaving certain things behind—the flashlight and bug dope and shoes. It would require going barefoot and relying on senses other than sight to feel my way through the darkness. It would mean letting go the belief that every single living thing in the big, black bag of night is out to get us.

Parade Season

PARADE SEASON begins when the weather turns summery and the first thundering boom from a bass drum floats through an open window. That's when we drop everything and hit the sidewalk running, more or less, to a four-four beat. There are parades on Memorial Day and the Fourth of July, interchangeable in their marching bands and convertible-borne politicians. These are celebrations that look backwards to the past, but my favorite parade, weeks earlier, is all about the future. On that day, the Saturday afternoon before Mother's Day, four blocks of Water Street are sealed off for the annual Doll and Pet Parade.

The commercial center of Eau Claire may have moved to malls on the outskirts of town, but Water Street remains the center of the city's nightlife—a row of narrow, two-story red-brick storefronts, cafes, and bars that cater mainly to the college crowd. For a few years one of the bars sponsored a Memorial Day Drag Race in which male patrons sprinted down the block in skirts and high heels until the physical toll of twisted ankles put an end to the event. The Doll and Pet Parade, which has lasted much longer, operates on roughly the same principle: allowing participants the chance to briefly be something they aren't.

Every year the Doll and Pet Parade has a different theme— "Storybook Characters" or "The Wild West"—but the prevailing motif is always youth, youth and innocence, because a certain of amount of innocence is required to march down the middle of a city street lined with strangers and see in those smiling, unfamiliar faces only encouragement.

The parade musters in the parking lot of a Holiday gas station where marchers are organized into categories, each led by a Boy Scout holding a placard: DOLLS & BUGGIES, PETS, WAGONS, BICYCLES, ROLLERBLADES & SKATEBOARDS. There's some last-minute costume adjusting and threading of crepe paper streamers through bicycle spokes before a fire truck, lights flashing, starts the procession, followed by a color guard from the American Legion. Then the whole unruly caravan of youth begins to move, pushing doll buggies and pulling wagons, down the double yellow line.

The first wave of marchers crosses Fifth Street past Roy's Barbershop and a former sports shop that's now a bar and a tanning parlor that used to be a pizzeria. For longtime residents, the parade offers a yardstick for how the city itself has changed. Storefronts change hands, go bust or burn down; there are now more black and brown faces in the parade as the city's population has grown more diverse over time, but what's most on display here is continuity. Since 1946, the first year of the Baby Boom, the Doll and Pet Parade has provided the city's youngest residents with their first experience of public life. "I was in it," says Pat Lokken, a parade organizer. "My children were in it. And now my grandchildren are in it."

The owner of The Joynt stands in the bar's doorway with his collie mix and watches the pet category troop past. Dogs outnumber cats and seem to enjoy being walked down the pavement on a leash; whereas the cage-bound cats look angry and betrayed. The same holds true of the children. The older ones relish the novelty of skateboarding down a normally busy street while the littlest towed in wagons look bewildered or frightened. Few notice the review stand atop a flatbed truck where the judges—a police officer, a city council member, a local TV personality—represent future career possibilities. I like watching the parade from curbside so that I'm eye level with the marchers and can see the thing from their perspective—its sheer enormity. One year the parade's theme was "It's a Small World," and the world it depicted looked no bigger or more threatening than our own neighborhood. France was a boy in a beret, Japan a white-faced girl in a kimono. My daughter, wearing a straw sombrero and carrying a plastic chicken, seemed to represent the entire southern hemisphere.

Of course, the real world is more complicated, and one task of parenthood is revealing that fact in small doses. Sometimes, however, children intuit this complexity on their own. Halfway through his first parade, our youngest decided the grinning adults lining the street were more strange than encouraging, and he began to cry. Reluctantly, I left the curb and hoisted the crying toddler to my hip. There was no easy retreat, so I joined the parade and started marching, an uncostumed stilt walker among the children, as we advanced toward the finish line and that inevitable future. The parade ended at Second Street where a DJ played a recording of "The Chicken Dance" and waited for the judges to award prizes. The middle-school marching bands had already dispersed, although some of the horn section waited in line for free ice cream. Cradling their plumed hats, they seemed reluctant to move on.

Memorial Days

ON THE FIRST LEG of a motorcycle trip out West, I shot past a white cross along an otherwise empty stretch of northern Montana. Farther down the road, two more crosses. The next day they were strung along my route at regular enough intervals to suggest Stations of the Cross. I learned to anticipate their next appearance: a hairpin curve or a precipitous hillside or a blunt bridge abutment. American Legion posts erect the white metal crosses as a highway safety measure, "a sobering reminder" to travelers of the dangers of the road. The dead don't play much of a role in this scheme except to locate the crosses with their untimely ends. In their stark whiteness, the crosses imply that there are limits even in a western landscape that's all possibility. Frankly, I found the metal crosses a dangerous distraction, especially if I was leaning into a curve and caught one in my peripheral vision. Their sheer anonymity left my imagination to fill in the blanks. A single cross on a flat stretch of two-lane was a drunken rollover. A pair of crosses on a curve: a tragic date. Three crosses: a head-on collision between a semi and a family returning home from Yellowstone. Passing a hillside where a staggering five white crosses were arranged in a pyramid, all I could picture were the Flying Wallendas screaming toward earth.

As I followed the Continental Divide south, the secondary roads worsened while the roadside crosses along them became more elaborate—and personal. They were made of wood and painted white as well as sky blue or pink and often wreathed in bright plastic flowers or a rosary and almost always inscribed with a name. Some were ornate as side altars, decorated with plaster statues or stuffed animals or a small American flag or sometimes all of these things. Most had a framed photograph of the departed—a face to put with the name. In this specificity, they were more crucifix than cross. They weren't intended as a warning to the living but as a memorial to the dead, that fellow traveler—Maria or Luis or Carlos—whose journey had abruptly ended here, at this very spot, beside these quaking aspens, this empty sky.

There is a tradition in the Southwest of the *descanso*, literally "place of rest," that commemorates the places where a funeral procession might pause on its way from churchyard to cemetery. As automobiles and highways opened up the world beyond the village, so did the practice of marking places where people died, thus extending the association, according to poet Rudolfo Anaya, "between the road, the interrupted journey, and death as a destination." The main difference between the white crosses of Montana and the *descansos* of New Mexico was the extent to which the latter took personal grief and made it public.

I don't remember seeing many roadside memorials in the Midwest, where mourning is limited to a few weeks beyond which grief is considered self-indulgent. But ever since returning from my motorcycle trip, I've been noticing objects along the roads: a state trooper's hat hung on a cross, a "ghost bicycle" painted entirely white and chained to a streetlamp, plaster angels and a child's pair of swim socks arranged beside a boat landing. Is it possible we're becoming less private in our sorrow, more Hispanic in our grief? I certainly hope so.

The Wisconsin Department of Transportation no longer outlaws roadside memorials but instead encourages the bereaved to channel their sorrow into its Adopt-A-Highway program. Picking up litter along a stretch of road named for the deceased may be a fine idea, but it's not exactly in the spirit of *descansos*, the implication being that grief alone is pointless unless tied to some useful act. I disagree. Roadside memorials remind us that not everyone dies at home in bed or wired into a hospital room; sometimes loved ones leave us in the midst of things, running an errand or going to work, and the object by the side of the road marks where they departed. And it's okay to remember the dead, not just once a year on a visit to the cemetery but at unexpected times and places, in the changing weather and turn of seasons.

Advice to Graduates

DISTINGUISHED COLLEAGUES, graduating seniors, proud parents and grandparents, friends, relatives, and insignificant others: I want to thank the administration for this opportunity to deliver today's commencement address, thereby saving the university whatever fees an outside speaker might have commanded. Having sat through my share of commencement speeches, I promise to deliver the parallel sentence structure and elaborate expressions of false hope you have every right to expect.

Today marks a beginning rather than an end, an end to the beginning, or maybe it's the beginning of the end. You are embarking on a journey, following in the steps of those who've gone before, closing one chapter in your life only to start another. I'm here today to share the ten steps to success. Actually, there are only three steps. But what is success? To some people, it's money or fame or influence. For me, it's standing on a big stage doling out advice to people I don't even know. Now is the time to take the tools you've been given and give back to others—but don't give back the tools. They're your tools. You paid for them. Remember that it takes a village. It takes all of us pulling together. It takes one to know one. So spread your wings and follow your dreams. Follow your bliss, whatever that is, and go boldly where no man has gone before. Follow the ushers at the end of the ceremony, per instructions, and be sure to write if you find work.

During your time at the university you may have read *Walden*, Henry David Thoreau's account of two years lived alone in a shack in the woods. Every American should read *Walden* if for no other reason than he or she may be called upon to deliver a commencement speech. From one bunting-lined dais to another, speakers are ransacking it for suitable epigrams. Somewhere a successful hedge-fund manager is leaning on a college podium and quoting Thoreau: "Our life is frittered away by detail. Simplify. Simplify."

A simple life might seem attractive at this point in your life. Why not head into the woods for some downtime? Why not just chill for a couple of years?

Well, I tried that advice. After graduating from college I moved to Alaska in a VW van and started building a log cabin, intending to live a simple life. But it's hard to build anything if you have no carpentry skills, and it's next to impossible to live off the land when you don't know how. What I learned is that even a simple life is exceedingly difficult. In the end, I did what many people do when they experience failure: I went to graduate school. In graduate school I learned that Thoreau wasn't saying avoid the world; he was saying avoid the trivial.

At this point in the commencement address, I'm contractually obliged to tell a joke or inspirational story that will allow me to pursue my chosen theme. In this regard I'm lucky, having built a career explaining other people's stories. The story I'd like to share is one most of you already know, and it's neither funny nor inspiring: the parable of the Prodigal Son. It is, however, a masterpiece of narrative compression. The younger son demands his portion and sets off to a far country where he wastes his inheritance in riotous living; then a famine strikes, and he's reduced to working as a hired man on a hog farm. All this in the opening sentences!

The rest of the story consists of three scenes, one for each of the principle characters—the father, the younger son, and his older brother—the nuclear family minus any females. The younger son returns and delivers his I'm-really-sorry speech. The father is so joyful at the prodigal's return that he throws him a party. For me the most poignant scene is when the older son hears music and has to learn from a servant that his good-for-nothing brother has returned. The old man tries to smooth things over by telling the older son, "rejoice for this thy brother was dead and has come to life; he was lost, and is found." All I can picture is the older brother thinking, "Yeah, well what about me?"

If you take the story as a religious allegory, which is certainly the way I've heard it in church every year of my life, there's only one meaning. The father represents God, whose perfect love forgives everything. But if you take the Prodigal Son as a story about people, which is how I read it, then there's no easy lesson, only the observation that life is complicated. It's complicated because even in a small family everyone has his own point of view. From the older brother's perspective, the father's indiscriminate love only makes things worse. (Which is certainly what Mom would say if she was in the story: "Dad the Enabler.") What makes the story interesting is its complexity, the way that it doesn't solve the problem it presents but only suggests a solution, one that is not without consequences.

There are two points I want to make. First, the *world* is complicated. You already know this, which is why you were reluctant to leave your seats when I said, "Spread your wings" a few moments ago and you just sat there because you know as well as I do how complicated things are going to get once you leave the building. The world is complicated, which leads to my second point: complexity is what makes life interesting. Presumably you learned this in college when you took five completely unrelated courses every semester. How crazy is that? You learned that subjects that appear simple to the uninitiated are worthy of the most intense study. Mainly you learned that there is always more to learn.

Live long enough, and you get to be all the characters in the parable—one year the footloose wanderer, the next a dutiful worker, and finally the bumbling father. That's the good news. The bad news is that eventually you become your parents. But how bad can that be?

So that's my wish for you, not a simple life but a full one. Go ahead and drift for a while. Move to California and live in a tent, but don't be afraid to complicate your life in the usual ways. As Zorba the Greek says in Nikos Kazantzakis's novel, "Wife, children, home, everything. The full catastrophe." Those obligations—domestic or otherwise—don't just connect you to the world. They are the world.

JUNE

Turtles

EARLY ONE SUMMER MORNING, driving over a swampy isthmus between lakes, I stopped to watch a turtle cross the road. It was a snapper, big as a washtub, hauling itself across two lanes of blacktop with a plodding, muscle-bound gait. It had a mossy, crenulated shell too small for its bulk and a head like a regulation football. The snapper moved at a slow, deliberate pace as if ignoring our presence would prevent us from noticing it. Fat chance. Traffic backed up in both directions, all of us idling in our air-conditioned shells to watch this prehistoric wonder cross the road. Here was a literal intersection of the human and natural worlds, and it made you want to stop and take notice. At least that's what I thought until someone in the opposite lane dashed into the road, grabbed the snapper by its serrated tail, and slung it into the bed of his pickup truck. Then he sped off in search, I suppose, of a big soup pot.

Of Wisconsin's eleven species of turtles, three are threatened or endangered and all are declining in number. Turtles are most vulnerable during the three weeks in June when females leave the water to lay their eggs on dry land, which the snapper I'd seen was undoubtedly attempting to do. It's illegal to take turtles from November to mid-July, though the law offers little protection against, say, a pair of belted radials. Now when I see turtles crossing pavement, I make a point of escorting them, dragging snappers by the tail and carrying the others at mid-shell, usually getting peed on for my efforts. I'm not being altruistic. I just like turtles.

Turtles look old in the same ways bald-headed babies do, the gaping mouth and grave aura of self-possession. They hiss if annoyed but otherwise keep mum, reacting to everything—even being dragged across a roadway—with the same Buster Keaton deadpan. Snapping turtles may bite if cornered on land, but in water they're as likely to surface gregariously in a knot of horrified swimmers just to check things out. What we perceive as stoicism in turtles may simply be a result of their lugging shelter on their backs; wherever a turtle finds itself, it's home. Some turtles, like the western painted, have a plastron, or bottom shell, so colorful and elaborately mottled, it could be a William Morris design. The plastron of the male wood turtle is concave to allow the male to mount a female; stacked one atop the other, a pair of amorous wood turtles resemble nothing so much as helmets mating.

Once a female turtle deposits the dozen or more Ping Pong–sized eggs in sun-warmed soil to incubate, half of her dangerous journey is over. But for eggs and hatchlings to come, the odds get even worse. Skunks, raccoons, and foxes are all proficient at digging out nests and eating the eggs. A long-term study of Blanding's turtles in Michigan found that nesting success rates (the percentage of eggs that hatched) declined from an average of 44 percent around 1980 to an average of just 3 percent in 1990. Of the hatchlings that make it out of the nest, few live long enough to reach the age of sexual maturity, seventeen to twenty years, to begin the process again. The Blanding's is one of the three Wisconsin species most on the brink, along with the wood and ornate box turtle. These aren't the sort of turtle people turn into soup but the one most likely to be collected as pets, especially by small boys.

Growing up in the suburbs, I considered turtles a stand-in for the rest of nature and couldn't resist taking one home whenever the opportunity presented itself. My favorite, picked up on a country road near a lake, had a black carapace, or upper shell, speckled with yellow spots and a hinged plastron that closed like a drawbridge for protection. It was, I realize now, a Blanding's turtle. I kept him (it seemed like a he) in a backyard enclosure made out of garden fence and fed him earthworms and raw hamburger. He made a docile if thwarted prisoner. Sometimes he'd extend his long, brontosaurus neck to peer over the fence, and I'd pet the back of his head, which felt warm and smooth like my grandfather's bald patch. One day the turtle was gone. He'd pushed aside the fence where it met the garage and escaped. Behind our house, a park sloped away to a divided highway and beyond that lay a wooded ravine with a stream at the bottom. Even if he managed to cross the first set of lanes, the turtle faced a wall-like curb, then more traffic. I hope he made it.

Act II

A COLLEAGUE OF MINE got married not so long ago in a city park on a hot summer afternoon. The park had plenty of other diversions, which meant that people not in the wedding party occasionally floated through the ceremony and there was a lot of chasing down of small children who were. When it was time, the bride and groom stepped onto a raised platform and the rest of us took seats in the surrounding amphitheater. The bride wore a traditional Hmong woman's wedding trousseau: black, turbanlike hat, white dress, and high heels that raised her height to almost five feet. Her fiancé, who was exceedingly tall and fair, also wore a traditional outfit—flared black trousers and beautifully embroidered vest—only on him it looked like a costume. Besides the two principals and the minister, there was a fourth person on the dais who translated the readings from English into Hmong. Any number of the bride's relatives could have performed this task, but the bride had pointedly chosen a friend who, like the groom, wasn't Hmong, as if to say: "Things change. This may look like a traditional ceremony, a fixed ritual in an ancient culture, but it isn't."

As the maid of honor launched into Paul's familiar epistle to the Corinthians—love is this, love is that—in perfect English, and the translator reworked those sentiments into a second language that I don't understand a word of, my mind began to wander. It wandered all the way to Grover's Corners. I'd recently seen a revival of *Our Town*, and now in the drowsy heat the wedding began to seem like an open-air production of the play. There was the minimalist staging, my brilliant colleague's transformation into

89

the mostly silent role of the Bride, the minister's way of narrating the action while inviting the audience to ponder its meaning—the Stage Manager's job in the play. I wouldn't have been surprised if Bride and Groom had mounted stepladders to exchange vows.

It's a bad habit of mine, this compulsion to translate real life into its arty equivalent. Of course, I've got this backwards. Thornton Wilder wrote a wedding scene that distills every wedding you've ever attended. In Act II of Wilder's play, entitled "Love and Marriage," George Gibbs, "the best baseball pitcher Grover's Corners has ever had," prepares to marry Emily Webb, the girl next door. But before the first notes of "The Wedding March" ring out, the audience is privy, through flashbacks, to the couple's nagging doubts. What frightens George and Emily, even though they've known each other all their lives, is change. There aren't many times in life when you're called upon to stand up in public and solemnly promise to do something until death. As the Stage Manager points out, marriage is the first step on a nonstop conveyor belt: "The cottage, the go-cart, the Sunday afternoon drives in the Ford, the first rheumatism, the grandchildren, the second rheumatism, the deathbed, the reading of the will . . ." Who wouldn't be scared?

The paradox of *Our Town* is that nothing ever seems to change in Grover's Corners, and yet the play constantly reminds cast and audience alike that we're all hitched to time's comet. When the stage lights come on after intermission for the third act, nine years have somehow streaked past. The stage props have been rearranged so that the church has become a cemetery on the top of a hill overlooking the town—"a windy hilltop" is how the script puts it. But I'm getting ahead of myself. In the real life here and now, the curtain was still rising on Act II.

If my colleague the Bride was nervous, she didn't show it. Born in a refugee camp in Thailand, she'd already faced down more change than Emily Webb could have ever imagined. She had mastered a new country and a new language and looked ready to take on the world if need be. Still, marriage is serious business predicated on the idea that there's no going backwards in life, only forward, and when she recited her vows in two languages, we all felt the gravitational pull.

Fawn

THE MORNING already heating up. A line of pickups stops along a two-track logging road. We put on neon orange traffic vests and march down the road until we're staggered two or three arm's lengths apart along an open field. On Talesha Karish's signal, we step into the brush and stride, heads down, through waist-high grass trying to stay in a straight line despite hidden stumps and overgrown berm piles. The field had been logged maybe a decade earlier and has grown back to wild raspberry brambles and pine saplings. A hundred yards in, the line pivots around the last person on the left and swings slowly back toward the road. None of us say much because we're all so intent upon the search, as if we're on an Easter egg hunt or attempting to recover a body.

Talesha, a project technician with the DNR, suddenly stops and holds up her hand. In a small, almost preadolescent voice she invites us to see what she's found. The field is still greening up and the dead grass perfectly camouflages the spotted, summer-red fawn curled in its bed. The fawn remains perfectly still even as we gather around, relying on its only defense—a lack of scent. Talesha pulls on white latex gloves and parts the grass. Only then does the fawn cry out, a drawn-out, heartbreaking note that sounds more like a baby doll than a human infant: *Maaaaa!*

Before examining the fawn, Talesha slips a blindfold over its eyes, which makes the animal look even more vulnerable, more like a hostage. Then she and another DNR employee weigh the fawn in a sling, 3.5 kilograms, and note the condition of hoofs and umbilicus to determine age. The fawn is no more than three days old. In another day or two, hoofs hardened, it would have run away. An elastic radio collar is placed around the fawn's slender neck to enable the researchers to monitor the animal's movements throughout the summer. Then everyone steps away and the fawn stumbles off in search of a doe that is undoubtedly hiding nearby.

The radio collar is ultimately designed to send a single, pithy message: *I'm dead. Come find me.* If the transmitter fails to move for an eight-hour period, it switches to "mortality mode," a speeded-up signal that alerts the researchers that the animal has either slipped the collar or, more likely, fallen to a predator. "Fawn recruitment" is what wildlife biologists call the number of deer born in the spring that manage to survive long enough to make themselves available for hunters to shoot in November. But little research has been done into which predators account for the most fawn mortality. That's the point of this study. Once the carcass is located, the researchers treat the kill site as a crime scene. Aside from tracks and scat, each predator leaves traces of its modus operandi. Black bears, for instance, often skin their prey, peeling a fawn's thin coat so it's inside out like a sock. Bobcats are meticulous, leaving only deep lacerations on the throat or back. Coyotes, on the other hand, leave a mess, tearing and ripping at a carcass, then burying any leftovers for later use. Of the thirty fawns radio collared in the summer of 2012, slightly more than half died from predation. Bears killed five, bobcat four, coyotes one, and one predation was undetermined.

Postmortem work can be depressing at times. The researchers once picked up a mortality signal from a fawn they'd collared only three days after rescuing it from a swamp in which it had become helplessly mired. They searched and searched and couldn't locate the collar even though the signal indicated they were standing right over it. Then someone spotted an antennae sticking out of the dirt where coyotes had cached the carcass.

In the Bible, the slaughter of innocents is the downside of the Christmas story; in whitetail deer, it's simple biology, an evolutionary defense mechanism. Deer evolved during the Pleistocene, an era dominated by super-predators, yet while the cave bear and saber-toothed tiger went extinct, deer survived as a species because of their ability to reproduce at a rate that could outrun losses from predation, disease, and starvation. A yearling doe is capable of producing a pair of fawns, sometimes triplets, even before her first birthday and subsequently every year of her life, a prolificacy that explains why hunters can kill half a million deer and Wisconsin's deer herd remains unchanged. It's the sort of mortality-driven birth rate that Katherine Anne Porter once described, in another context, as the "grim and terrible race of procreation."

It's hard to fault predators for their role in the scheme of things, yet many Wisconsin hunters have done just that, blaming a decline in the deer harvest on the state's resurgent wolf population rather than their own methodical killing. The Fawn Recruitment Study is an attempt to bring science to bear on game management, though it's unclear whether science has much sway when hunters see fewer deer in the woods and automatically hear the ominous French horn section of Prokofiev's *Peter and the Wolf*

In the afternoon we bushwhack through a hot and buggy woods at the end of a muddy road. Talesha is tracking a VIT (vaginal inserted transmitter) signal that had been placed in a captured doe last January. The VIT is temperature sensitive so it starts transmitting when a fawn is born and the VIT drops to the ground. Since the VIT has only a half-mile signal radius, it has to be nearby. Finally one of the volunteers spots the bright orange VIT, which one of the researchers described as "the size of a tampon," on the leaf-strewn ground. Its plastic covering has been partially chewed. The doe had also eaten the afterbirth to eliminate any scent. But neither doe nor fawn is anywhere to be found.

Holding a palm-sized GPS, Talesha leads us through the forest. We loop over the same brushy hillside, walking a grid, exactly as a sow bear might do if she knows fawns are on the ground. We find trillium turning pink in the filtered sunlight. We find bear tracks in the muddy road, nine ruffed grouse eggs in a nest, and a heart-shaped Mylar balloon. We find wood ticks—lots of them—on our socks and trousers, but no fawn. The afternoon is winding down. Talesha finally calls a halt to the search, and we begin the long hike back to the cars. Either the newborn fawn has reunited with its mother and wandered far from this hillside or else it's been carried off by something else. Does it matter which? It's like the old conundrum of a tree falling in a woods if there's no one around to hear it. Without a radio collar, the fawn has slipped back into the usual state of anonymity, that place where animals live and die without our knowing even the slightest thing about them.

The Same River

THE LAST TIME I canoed the North Fork of the Flambeau was a scouting trip the week before deer season when a snowstorm suddenly poured out of the gray sky. Big wet flakes fell, piling up on gunwales and thwarts—every surface, in fact, but the dark river itself. The canoe drifted into what seemed a black-and-white movie. When a bald eagle dropped from a pine bough, it flapped heavily downstream, wings beating black-white, black-white.

Seven months later, on my first fishing trip of the year, the same river is translucent and light-shot and so steeply banked in greenery it might have headed in the Emerald City of Oz. Given the number of rivers within a reasonable distance that I *haven't* canoed, it might seem feckless to return year after year to the same one, but the North Fork remains my idea of a northern river: cobbled bottom, big white boulders in midstream, tangled pine spars leaning out from the banks. If I had to invent a river from scratch, it would look like the North Fork. While no rapids intersect this stretch, the drop in gradient is still noticeable, especially when the river jogs east and you look down the long corridor of water into the crowns of white pines.

The ten-mile run between Oxbow and the County W bridge takes half a day, longer if I bring a spinning rod, it having the same effect on the canoe's progress as dragging a sea anchor. Growing up in the dismal shadow of Motor City, my fishing opportunities were limited except in the public library, where I'd pore over books that divided my attention between freshwater species and the glowing, phosphorescent monsters of the Mariana Trench.

The book I read most devoutly was Sid Gordon's *How to Fish from Top to Bottom,* which offered the sensible advice that a bathysphere isn't necessary if one can read the surface of the water. Since riffles and boils give away underwater structures where fish may hide, I was drawn early on to rivers rather than lakes. This was all before fishing became a branch of applied electronics. Understanding where a fish might be as opposed to verifying it is there on a sonar screen is the difference between the essential mystery of sport and attempts to stack the deck.

While a new river holds the promise of the unknown, paddling the same river is a form of time travel, seesawing the canoeist back and forth between the present and trips past. Floating down the North Fork one summer with my daughter in the bow, we spotted what appeared to be a dead fish at the bottom of a rocky pool. It was a sleeping catfish, long as my arm, and as our canoe passed overhead it slowly tail-finned into deeper water. Late this afternoon when I reach the rocky pool, I'm a little disappointed to find the sleeping catfish isn't there. Somehow it's become a fixture in my memory of that spot. Did it fishtail into the depths two summers ago or four? The river works that way—every recollection another reminder of time elapsed. On the other hand, the North Fork itself has remained so constant over the years that it's possible to sustain the opposite illusion: that nothing has changed, that the river loops around in a tight space-time continuum on which all my previous trips are somehow connected, and if I just paddle harder, I might catch my younger self bobbing around the next bend.

The sun has sunk into the trees by the time the river divides itself around Babbs Island, with the deeper channel running along the west bank. I once lost a nice smallmouth here when a muskie ripped it from a trailing stringer as a kind of toll. How long ago was that? I've stopped casting by now and pull hard to make the bridge takeout by dark. Dusk always brings out the inner account, the nagging voice in my head that reckons hours spent against the general pointlessness of fishing. Ahead, a car rumbles across the yet-unseen bridge. The noise spooks a bald eagle, which drops from its perch across the river and flies at an angle downstream, wings beating black-white in the fading light.

Cow Shed

LAST WINTER the old cow shed on my in-laws' farm collapsed from the weight of snow. Technically it was a *loafing shed,* though I never heard anyone call it that. An outbuilding with three walls and a slanting tin roof, it offered the cattle shelter from heavy fall rains and oppressive summer sun. The shed also formed a good chunk of corral fence that would now have to be replaced. The network of fences nearest the barn is laid out to form concentric circles of confinement, the better to move cattle. When calves need to be separated from the rest of the herd so they can be inoculated or loaded to market, they're first driven from the cow yard to the smaller corral and finally ushered into a little holding pen. Last winter's heavy snow had caused two timbers holding up the shed roof to buckle, so all that's left is a sagging tangle of old boards, bent tin roofing, and a big hole to plug.

The first order of business before we can build a new fence is to disassemble the old shed and haul it away. Once the tin sheets are pried off, the plank roof resembles the hull of an ark that's run aground. My late father-in-law ran the farm with a Depression-era sensibility that meant nothing was thrown away if it might conceivably be useful down the road, including any nondimensional lumber we could savage from older buildings to use as fencing. If he was still alive, no doubt I'd be pulling nails and stacking the boards for some distant future instead of hauling them to the burn pile.

What remains of the corral fence once the cow shed is removed is a haphazard affair, cobbled together over time and constantly in need of repair. The oldest sections are made of lichen-covered oak timbers and rough-sawn palings that look as if they survived Noah's Flood but were nailed up only a dozen years ago. On a farm, fences don't just hold in livestock, they hold back chaos. Nature is always pressing in with weeds and trees, ready to take back whatever ground had been gained. My father-in-law used to move from machine to machine, plugging holes in his fence line as fast as they appeared, throwing corrugated tin and even sections of an old cattle feeder into the breach. The man was Sisyphus on a skid loader.

Now that my father-in-law is gone, ownership of the farm has passed to his half-dozen grown children. In a sense, what we're operating here is a collective farm, and it gives you a real appreciation for why the Soviet Union failed. There's little personal incentive for working hard and no end of criticism if you screw up. Farm meetings descend inevitably into family encounter sessions where everyone airs their grievances. Since nobody wants to act on his or her own initiative for fear of doing something wrong, we're mainly in maintenance mode. A cousin rents the cropland and pasturage, and it's his cattle we're repairing the corral to hold. He's the real farmer.

I've volunteered to rebuild the corral fence because it's within my narrow skill range and because I love being here. I love the pungent smell of burdock and lamb's quarters that take over when cattle aren't around to crop them. I love being useful in obvious ways, working with my hands instead of my mouth. And I love the chance to work with the next generation, in this case my niece's boyfriend, Andy, an ex-Marine and Iraq War veteran now deployed with a post-hole digger. We use the old post holes if we can find them; otherwise it means chopping through the limestone crust with a sharp iron bar. On a century farm, you're always following in someone's footsteps.

Cattle should "flow" when moving to or from the corral, so we lay out the new fence to avoid sharp corners where the cows could bunch up. We set the treated posts ten feet apart, backfill with gravel, and tamp down until the posts feel as solid in the ground as tree stumps. Then we attach wire cattle panels to a framework of two by sixes and two by fours spanning the posts. As my father-in-law liked to say, a fence only has to *look* sturdy to keep a cow from testing her weight against it. He knew all about the psychology of cows, but I want this new fence to last at least as long as the old one did.

After we finish and the tools are put away, Andy goes home for supper while I invent reasons to hang around a little longer. I clean up scrap lumber and survey the day's work from different vantage points. From a distance, some of our mistakes are painfully evident: posts that are uneven and boards not exactly plumb. So I rev up the chainsaw one more time and cut the tops of the posts to a uniform height because my father-in-law liked them that way.

JULY

Rodeo

"A RUNNING HORSE," the director John Ford once wrote, "remains one of the finest subjects for a movie camera." Running horses were certainly the main attraction in the Westerns I grew up watching on television: a few terse words, some gunplay, then horses galloping right to left across the screen, alone or in bunches, their hooves raising small, funnel-shaped clouds of dust. Of course, my appreciation of horses at this point was purely theoretical. The romance pretty much ended the first time I sat on one at summer camp and the nag attempted to scrape me off with a gatepost. After that, I just didn't see the point of horses, not in the Midwest anyway.

My wife, on the other hand, grew up riding horses and, despite being thrown on occasion, maintains affection for the beasts, which is why we're sitting high in the bleachers at the Stanley Rodeo. Stanley isn't the West. It's not even western Wisconsin. It's a small town in the heart of dairy country, the other major employers being an ethanol plant and a state prison. Yet the stands are crowded with people, many of whom have traded in feed caps for cowboy hats, at least for tonight's show. As John Ford—who left Maine to make cowboy pictures in Southern California—understood, the West is first and foremost a state of mind.

The rodeo predates the Western movie and managed to outlast it in large part by refusing to change. While Hollywood attempted to reboot the genre by turning out anti-Westerns in which the cowboy hero turns out to be a psychopath, the rodeo never strayed from its essential vision of rugged self-sufficiency presented without the slightest trace of irony.

The Stanley rodeo begins with a huge American flag unfurled as we all stand and sing the national anthem. Then an announcer on horseback charges into the arena wearing a stiff white shirt and a black Stetson the size of a manta ray. In a somber Kansas baritone, he recites the Cowboy Prayer: *We pray that you will guide us in the Arena of Life. As cowboys we don't ask for any special favors. We don't ask to draw around a chute-fighting horse or to never break a barrier. Nor do we ask for all daylight runs . . .* After the prayer, he introduces Miss Rodeo Wisconsin, who, the announcer notes, has recently graduated with a degree in elementary education and a minor in Spanish (useful if she meets any *vaqueros*).

The first event, bareback bronc riding, only confirms my initial impression of horses as untrustworthy when a succession of cowboys are dislodged by animals with names like Crazy Eight, Showtime, and Good Luck. Bolting out of the chute, the bronc contracts itself, then suddenly releases, snapping the rider back and forth until a hat flies into the air, followed a second or two later by its owner. Most of the bronc riders are from west of the Mississippi, and the one in-state rider gets a thunderous round of applause as his name is announced, only to bite the dust soon after clearing the chute. Apart from the obvious risk of spinal compression and hyperextended joints, riders face the potential of getting trampled or dragged if a hand gets caught in the rigging. As a precaution most wear a leather flak jacket and, one hopes, a cup. Tonight only a few hold on for the required eight seconds, swinging their free arm to counterbalance the horse's gyrations. The real heroes of this event are the two pickup men, who race out as the buzzer sounds and bracket the bronc long enough for the rider to slide onto the back of one of their horses.

The lunacy of bull riding aside, most rodeo events derive from everyday ranch or farm chores involved in handling rough stock. It is part of the American genius to transform such tasks as calf roping into a competition simply by adding the elements of speed and a cash prize. The calf gets a head start across the arena before the rider pursues at full gallop while twirling a lasso. I don't understand the physics of throwing a rope forward at a running object while simultaneously moving forward oneself, but timing has to be part of it. A number of ropers either don't close the gap quickly enough to fire their lariat or miss the calf. When a cowboy is on target, he jumps off his horse, throws the calf to the ground, and ties three of the animal's legs together with a "pigging string" he carries in his teeth. Then he throws his hands in the air to signal he's completed his tie. It is the same motion a certain NFL linebacker pantomimes whenever he sacks a quarterback, except the successful roper doesn't have a million-dollar contract or do a celebratory end-zone dance. He just picks his hat off the ground, swats it against his jeans to shake off the dust, and climbs back in the saddle.

Before machines took their place, horses did much of the work of farming as late as the 1940s. My wife's father grew up when threshing crews required a dozen or more horses, and he could still throw a decent lariat long after there was a reason to. By the time I showed up, he did most of his farming from the seat of a tractor or a front loader, not a saddle. A single horse remained on the place, a white-faced gelding, aloof as a ghost. Unlike other farm animals, it was exempt from work or doing much of anything other than standing on a windy hillside looking iconographic. Sometimes when I'd come down to help separate cattle, chasing calves around the corral on foot and making cowboy sounds, the horse would amble by and exchange looks with my father-in-law.

Horsemanship isn't the rodeo's only draw. What the rodeo celebrates is a type of physical courage missing from football or other professional "games" because it derives from what used to be considered work—handling livestock. There's also an attitude that translates well in the rural Midwest. To "cowboy up" is to absorb physical punishment without complaint and only a slim chance of financial reward; it's saying, in effect, *I can take whatever you dish out without whining about it.* The physical toll of farming is no less real than the battering that goes on at a rodeo, except that it's drawn out over a lifetime with no thunderous applause at the end. So it must be particularly satisfying in dairy country to take the evening off and sit in the stands where that kind of stoicism looks more heroic than foolish.

Motorcycle

STEVE MCQUEEN on a motorcycle rides toward a distant line of blue mountains. For a moment, World War II fades from the wide screen and all that remains is Mr. Cool on a Triumph 650 tooling across the Bavarian countryside. He roars past loden-green forests and picturesque villages with orange tiled roofs. Pursued by the German army, he quits the pavement and heads cross-country toward Switzerland. Just before the mountains looms a barbed-wire fence. The Swiss border! McQueen ascends a ramp-like hill, rolls on the throttle, and is airborne.

That's all I remember of the movie: the motorcycle scenes. I was fifteen, and the only people in my neighborhood who rode motorcycles were the Bacon brothers, identical twins with matching duck-ass haircuts and intimidating sneers. They owned explosively loud British bikes whose thundering racket preceded any sighting of the twins. I remember racing to our kitchen window to see the brothers hunched over their machines, shirttails flying, as they roared past our house on an errand of no good. At sixteen I bought a little 160cc bike and practiced popping wheelies in my girlfriend's driveway. Weekends we'd sit at the drive-in watching a different sort of motorcycle movie, one in which a band of misfits descends upon a small town and disassembles it. At a certain point in the mayhem, I'd tell my girlfriend how much she looked like Nancy Sinatra.

Thirty years later I bought a much bigger bike and enrolled in a motorcycle course at the local vocational-tech school, practicing controlled skids and figure-eight formations on the same expanse of blacktop where other students learned to drive eighteen-wheelers. Our instructor began each class with a simple koan: "The clutch is your little buddy. And what do you do if you get into trouble?" To which we'd all sing: "Give our little buddy a squeeze!" Half the class was made up of middle-aged men like myself who'd owned a motorcycle as a teenager and hoped to re-capture a little magic from those days. At the completion of the course, we were awarded certificates of instruction and obliged to sit through a mandatory film on organ donation.

A hot summer weekend. Highway 35, the Great River Road, throbs with motorcycle traffic, heavy chrome cruisers ridden by peo-ple dressed as if bound for the Pirate's Ball, their black leather vests and do-rags creating an effect quite unlike the unstudied menace of the Bacon brothers. A few riders extend a gloved hand from their handlebar grip in the biker's salute, but most don't. We're headed in opposite directions, imagining different movies, as it were.

I no longer connect motorcycling to the thuggish dreams of adolescence. The point isn't to make a noisy spectacle of one's self but to see the countryside, which is why I prefer two lanes to four and gravel roads to almost anything. So my friends and I are setting off on the Trans-Wisconsin Adventure Trail, a 600-mile traverse of the state from the Illinois border to Lake Superior. We'd found the route on a website that showed pictures of motorcyclists spattering down muddy forest roads and occasionally through small streams. Some of the riders wore "armored" jackets and long-visored motocross helmets that made them look like knights-errant.

On the second day of the trip, we cross the Wisconsin River and climb into ridge-and-coulee country. You accelerate up a hill to blue sky, then downshift into the next green valley. The landscape reveals itself in successive zones of temperature and light, the damp smell of a pine forest giving way to sunlit pastures and the tang of fermenting manure. We follow the Kickapoo River through one red brick town after another—Steuben, Barnum, Soldiers Grove—a few city blocks, then more farmland. We're seeing an earlier version of the Midwest, a rural land of small farms and steepled churches where narrow roads connect little towns instead of bypassing them.

J.B. Jackson, the great cultural geographer, used to ride a BMW motorcycle between annual lectureships at Harvard and Berkeley to keep track of changes in the American landscape. The motorcyclist, he observed, enters "a world of flowing movement, blurred lights, rushing wind; he feels the surface beneath him, hears the sound of his progress, and has a tense rapport with his vehicle." Riding on two wheels makes you concentrate not only on the rushing landscape but the road itself, alert to surface changes as crushed limestone gives way soft pea gravel and your rear tire begins fishtailing toward the shoulder. At such unexpected moments, you achieve the sort of "tense rapport" that leaves your hands welded to the grips.

My companions all ride quiet, German-speaking BMWs. My bike is a 650cc, single-cylinder "thumper" with a drilled exhaust pipe that plays gear shifts on an ascending scale whenever there's a chance to open the throttle, which isn't often. Over the engine racket, I keep a running monologue in my head of passing wildflowers—Turk's cap, bee balm, chicory, brown-eyed Susans, Queen Anne's lace—so I can write them down later.

It's haying weather, the air hot and shimmery. On every hilltop, farmers are cutting or raking or baling hay. Somewhere north of

Soldiers Grove, the tractors are replaced by teams of draft horses reined in by men on foot wearing beards and broad-rimmed hats. You know you've crossed into Amish country when the wavering line down the middle of the pavement turns out to be road apples.

"Out for a ride?" Mrs. Yoder asks. She looks out the window of her farmhouse bakery to four motorcycles recumbent on kickstands in the yard. We buy a caramel coffee cake, and she inquires where we were heading. "Sounds nice," she says as if Lake Superior lay over the next ridge.

Next morning, rain pelts the parking lot outside our motel and there's a line at the waffle machine. Dolefully shoveling down Mrs. Yoder's coffee cake, we watch the weather channel on TV, where the storm appears as a violet blob tracking east across the Upper Great Lakes. Long after the last minivan has departed, we glide out of the puddled parking lot and race through central Wisconsin on section line roads that run in cardinal directions straight as arrows. We're in the heart of America's Dairyland, where plastic-wrapped hay bales line the fields and the highest points around are silos. The only things missing from this scene are green pastures dotted with black-and-white cows. Where are the Holsteins? On the larger dairy operations they're in confinement buildings, milked and fed under a single roof. We still see cows pastured on smaller, traditional dairy farms, but many of the grassy fields we pass are unfenced and empty.

North of Highway 64 the woods press in from both sides of the road. The farm fields get smaller and rockier, and most have an island of picked stone in the center where a few trees have gotten purchase. It's like seeing Wisconsin history flowing backwards— cows replaced by trees, pastures reverting to woods. For the rest of the day we're tunneling through forests, the only other traffic an occasional logging truck.

The last leg of the trip is on numbered forest roads that lead to the Moquah Barrens, an outwash plain of jack pine and sand and the final barrier to the lake. The sand runs so deep that I have to frog-walk the motorcycle in first gear through some draws to keep it upright and hope I don't burn out the clutch. When we finally emerge from the barrens, it's onto a narrow ribbon of blacktop that climbs steadily to the Lake Superior height of land, from which can be seen a faint blue line of hills. The North Shore! The rest is downhill. What fun to finally open the throttle and hear the big single's rising vibrato as I accelerate through the gears, the bike picking up speed until it feels like I'm hurtling down a steep ramp and about to go airborne.

Dobsonfly

WHAT FIRST APPEAR as sprinkles from a cloudless sky turn out to be insects peppering my car's windshield as we drive north. The shimmery air is fairly alive with them, midges and gnats and something yellow that goes splat. By the time we cross the bridge and roll to a stop beside the cabin, the front bumper has grown a five o'clock shadow of bug remains and colorful bits of butterfly wings decorate the grill. I'd feel bad about the carnage if not for the sheer abundance of insects this time of year.

Midsummer marks an apex of sorts on the calendar and fecundity may well be the word for it, high noon on nature's biological clock, time for every creature to get busy mating or hatching or feeding on some other creature. The river itself is manic with activity. Last month swallows appeared and started building mud-and-waddle nests under the bridge. Now they swarm from those nests to feed on mayflies that have eluded the smallmouth bass, which are themselves relentlessly pursued by a great stalking heron.

Upon arrival, one of my son's rituals when he was younger was to overturn every good-sized rock or loose chunk of firewood to see what lived underneath. He was stalking garter snakes and red-back salamanders, anything wild he could hold wriggling in his hand. One summer when the shrieking commenced, I ran over to see what he'd uncovered. It was a bug—the biggest, ugliest bug I'd ever seen, four inches of rubbery brown insect with veined, transparent wings like a cicada's folded over its abdomen. But the wings made up only half its considerable body length. The rest was head and thorax and wavering antennae and—this is the horrible part—great tusklike mandibles protruding from its head.

"Gross!" my son said and replaced the rock.

It was a male dobsonfly, *Corydalis cornuta*, and its days were numbered. The dobsonfly didn't have long to live not because any of us planned to flatten it, but because it was in the last stage of a long and complicated life cycle. The dobsonfly is the final incarnation of a creature that begins as a hellgrammite, a favorite of bass fishermen and no great beauty itself. After three years of living underwater, usually in the swiftest part of a stream, the hellgrammite hauls itself ashore, crawls under a rock, and begins to pupate. It's the reverse of the Ugly Duckling story, for what emerges a few days later, usually at night, is a dobsonfly. The wings and fierce-looking mandibles make it look horrific, except the mandibles aren't for feeding; they're for grasping a female. They're literally love handles, the better for holding onto Ms. Dobsonfly, and the wings are for finding her. The male has only a handful of days to locate a female and mate before dying. Then the female lays her eggs by the thousands on a rock or branch overhanging the river, and when they fall into the river the whole sequence begins again. We'd missed the bulk of this performance and stumbled onto the last act only by accident.

Lately I've been visiting a website called "What's That Bug?" where people post photographs of insects that creep them out to be identified. In July these are overwhelmingly dobsonflies, sometimes posed beside a quarter or a house key for scale. Collectively the pictures suggest an Old Testament plague. One inquiry begins: "We attend Bible college, are from ages 18–24 and yet we're freaked out by this thing that looks like it could eat your soul . . . P.S. Wow! God has creativity."

"Dear scared students," comes the reply. "Evolution and Natural Selection truly are wondrous."

None of the writers admit to squashing a dobsonfly. On the contrary, they all seem exhilarated by an encounter with something so "strange." Repulsion and wonder are the flip sides of each other; either can be taken as evidence for a Grand Design in Nature or else the whirligig of chance. Both are close cousins to awe, and awe is what we're seeking when we turn over rocks. It's why I stand beneath the yard light after dinner watching the swirling cone of bugs, so many brief lives briefly illuminated—like stars, like distant worlds brought into view.

Pine River

THE PINE is part of a network of alliterative rivers in northeastern Wisconsin that includes the Pike, Popple, and Peshtigo—as if the cartographer had gotten stuck on the letter *P*. These rivers head in the same high plateau of lakes and swamps that give rise to the Chippewa and Wisconsin, but while those big rivers flow westward in broad, flat swaths, the *P* rivers plunge in the opposite direction, descending the plateau like a row of steep, white staircases to the Michigan border. They also drop quickly after spring runoff, so the canoe guidebooks warn of low water after May. This was the second week of a blistering July, but then, we're optimists.

We didn't reach the campground until after dark, rolling across a smooth wooden bridge after miles of loose gravel and startled deer. We set up the tent in the car's headlights and then walked back to the bridge to check out the river. In the moonlight the road shone lighter than the trees on either side. At mid-span, we could hear the river without seeing it. When I played a flashlight downstream, the beam fell on what appeared to be a field of stone.

"Looks low," my friend said.

Next morning I crawled on hands and knees from the tent to find the campground filled with sunlight and pines and a river rushing just beyond a screen of alders. We'd skipped the Pine's upper branches to launch mid-river at Chipmunk Rapids. The rapids were hardly that, just a little rock garden below the wooden bridge that smelled of creosote in the rising heat. We walked the canoe into the water, pointed the bow downstream, and the let the current carry us away.

The Pine narrowed, bare cedars leaning overhead, and we fell into the easy rhythm of paddling: a few strokes, a comment.

"Rivers are more fun than lakes," my friend said, "because they have, you know, a narrative."

He talks this way because he is a novelist. He'd just completed a grueling twenty-three-city tour to promote his latest novel and was looking for a little relaxation and fishing. I knew the narrative he had in mind for the Pine River because I had sold it to him sight unseen over the phone as one might sell investment property in central Florida. The promised river was deep and smooth running and practically paved with trout.

"This is certainly a wild river," he said over his shoulder from the bow. "But where are the trout?"

None had risen to our spinners despite the flailing we were giving the water. A cloud of sulphur butterflies hovered over a mud bank. In the clear brown water I spotted the skeleton of a small deer.

The upper Pine bisects national forest land before entering Wisconsin Wild River status, a linear buffer against the incursions of logging and summer cottages. The shoreline is stiff with white pine and cedar, though what keeps the river wild is its own loopy disposition toward sudden falls and grade III rapids.

We came up on the first of these, a curlicue of granite and whitewater in two pitches called Snaketail Rapids. Since we didn't plan to run anything larger than a riffle, we beached the canoe above the first pitch and began portaging our gear. At the same time, young men in three bright red canoes came yahooing down the river and shot into the rapids. Through the trees we occasionally heard shouts and caught flashes of red. Only two canoes were still afloat below the last rapids, the third having caught on a rock and spilled its load of reckless youth. But the swimmers looked none the worse for wear as we pitched our heavy packs on the ground and doubled back for more.

Despite feeder streams below the rapids, the Pine got shallower and shallower as if it had sprung a leak. Soon all that remained was a thin sheet of water that glared sunlight and hid any number of rocks. After the canoe bottomed out on the umpteenth rock, we got out and lined it downstream.

"Nobody should attempt this river," the novelist said ruefully, "without knowing at least four verses of 'Song of the Volga Boatmen.'"

We camped above Meyers Falls where the woods opened into a field of columbine. After a supper, pointedly not of trout, we opened warm cans of beer and stretched out by the fire. Through the birches the surface of the river turned lilac, then darkened with the sky. Smoke climbed a dim shaft of light above the fire.

The first recorded observations of the Pine River country are those of Captain Thomas Jefferson Cram, United States Topographical Engineer, who surveyed the border between Michigan and Wisconsin Territory in the autumn of 1840. Triangulating around Sandy Lake, the survey party men were approached by Indians, who informed them that the land they were pulling a surveyor's chain across belonged to the Katakittekow Band of Chippewa.

The next day Chief Cashaosha arrived in the surveyors' camp and, after parlaying and receiving gifts, granted Cram passage through his country. Cram estimated the Katakittekow at one hundred men, women, and children. They summered on an island in Lac Vieux Desert and in winter hunted along the *Muskos Sepe,* or Pine River, where deer were said to be especially thick.

In the morning the novelist and I portaged around the falls and then ditched our canoe a mile downriver. We hitchhiked back to the car, retrieved our canoe, and drove on to Florence, the county seat. Beside the Romanesque-style courthouse stands a plaque commemorating Captain Cram's visit to the area. No mention is made of his host, Chief Cashaosha.

After replenishing our beer supply, we made plans to drive across the border to the Upper Peninsula and canoe the Paint River, which, I'd been assured, is practically paved with trout. That, of course, is another story.

AUGUST

Water Park

MY CHILDREN LEARNED TO SWIM in a tea-colored river with a lazy current and sandy bottom but also hidden drop-offs that changed every year and left me a nervous wreck. Once a summer, though, we'd pack a picnic lunch in the car along with a few neighborhood kids, drive to Wisconsin Dells, and spend an entire day at a water park. At the admission gate we'd exchange money for plastic wristbands, splash on sunscreen, then hotfoot it along the baking pavement to an age-appropriate ride. At first this meant the baby pool and long inner-tube rides on a circular canal called the Endless River, where the current was fixed and the dazzling blue water held no drop-offs. As the kids grew they graduated to more vertiginous water slides, including one advertised as "ten stories up and five seconds down" and which my son pronounced the perfect wedgie machine. In the drowsy afternoon my wife and I would rendezvous at the Tiki Bar to drink cold beer and listen to someone make a fool of himself singing "Ring of Fire" to a karaoke machine. Oh sweet summertime!

This alternating pattern of river and water park became a fixture in our summers, a means of having it both ways—nature as well as human nature. Each had its own attractions. The river had tadpoles and heron tracks and the possibility of turtles. But at the water park, the smell of fried food at the concession stands blended with the scent of chlorine and SPF 30 into a strange chemistry that just smelled like summer, and when the wave pool's artificial surf lifted a crowd and they let out a collective *whoop!,* my heart would too.

One stifling July I was talking to another writer about the heat, naturally, and since I'd just come from a water park I suggested she might enjoy one herself.

"I can't imagine!" she replied in her languorous, movie-star voice—a voice that suddenly made sliding down a plastic flume on one's fanny no longer seem fun but a lapse in judgment.

"No really," I insisted, "you've got to try Congo Bongo!"

It's pointless talking water parks to the uninitiated. Tell them you spent a happy afternoon floating the Endless River, and they'll smile sideways, wise to the fact that the Endless River isn't a river at all but a concrete moat with a current that shuts down at closing time. Tell them about the ten-story speed slide that turned your baggy swim trunks into a thong, and they'll tell you it's an imitation of a waterfall, a consumer-driven fake, a simulacrum!

Well, sure. It's like revealing that the stilt walker in the Fourth of July parade really isn't the World's Tallest Man. The only common denominators between rivers and water parks are water and gravity, and it hardly matters to the human body on a hot summer's day whether these forces are natural or contrived. The *whoop* is the same. A river offers solitude, but a water park is a lesson in democracy. I once stood on a switchback of wooden stairs leading to the next waterslide sandwiched between an Amish family (bearded men in cut-off trousers and pale women in bloomers) and a contingent of skinheads in low-rider trunks and spider-web tattoos. We waited patiently to ascend the stairs, all of us dripping wet and grinning like madmen. Only the lifeguards at the top, most of them foreign students with nametags that read Rudolpho or Ivana or Horst, looked bored behind their sunglasses and zinc oxide as they'd nod and send another American body whooshing down the chute. They'd seen it all—endomorphs and meso-morphs, the sleek and the hairy, the boxered and the thonged—a nation in the flesh.

At the river, my kids would beg for horseplay, to be dunked or catapulted off my shoulders—behavior that would warrant a whistle at the city pool. But Rudolpho or Ivana or Horst hardly ever blew a whistle because the water park was all about horseplay, all about ingenious devices for plunging people in the water and making a big splash.

Sadly, inevitably, the time comes when most of us blow the whistle on ourselves. The bright, sensory pleasures of childhood suddenly grow dim or appear crass and inauthentic, and we become paralyzed by self-consciousness. It's one more version of the Expulsion from Paradise, only self-directed. This is what happened to my daughter the summer before she left for college, the same college where the writer with the movie star voice taught. We were packing the car for the annual trip to the water park when she elected to stay home, dismissing the excursion with a cool irony. But her brother, younger and less of an ironist, went along and seemed to enjoy himself. He wore his bright blue plastic wristband for weeks afterward until it faded to white and finally fell off.

Sailing

CLIMBING UP THE COMPANIONWAY of a sailboat berthed at the Chicago Yacht Club, coffee cup in hand, I had arguably the best view in the city. I'd fallen asleep the night before listening to a vaguely middle-European, computer-generated baritone on the marine weather channel relentlessly forecasting a new round of storms. Now another storm was blowing in from the southwest, shrouding the Sears Tower in gray flannel. Soon the city skyline disappeared into a cloud. So I went back into the galley and drank coffee and listened to the drumbeat of rain on the roof.

When the storm let up, we slipped dock lines and motored out of the harbor and past the breakwater with the Loop at our backs. Dale Peters let out sail and we headed north along the coast at seven and a half knots. The most direct route to the Mackinaw Straits, the one Dale takes in the yearly Chicago to Mackinac Race, is a beeline up the middle of Lake Michigan, but this wasn't a race and we were taking a leisurely course more in keeping with the name of our ship. *Zig-Zag* is a sleek, white, thirty-five-foot sprit boat of the J-109 class. Her owner, a friend of Dale's, had brought her to Chicago to race in a regatta. We would sail her as far as Mackinac Island, where the owner would take delivery for the final leg of the trip to her home berth in Bayfield.

Having read Joshua Slocum's *Sailing Alone around the World* and Rockwell Kent's *N by E,* I occasionally dipped into their reservoir of nautical language. If for instance someone put so many drinks *down the hatch* that he was *three sheets to the wind,* I might say that I didn't care for the *cut of his jib*—whatever a jib was. But when we took turns steering the four-foot wheel, my lack of sailing experience became obvious. I'd drift off course, then wildly overcorrect. My steering problem was the result of focusing on the digital compass above the cabin rather than on some fixed point on the horizon. The horizon, however, had largely disappeared. We'd slipped into a fog that reduced visibility to three or four boat lengths. Off Racine Reef, we heard a foghorn and then a fainter horn, like an echo, from a freighter that probably had picked us up on radar. Somewhere off my left shoulder lived 11 million people, though for all I could see we might have been sailing up the Aleutian Chain toward the Pribilof Islands.

By early evening the fog lifted and Milwaukee floated into view, hovering above the horizon like a city in a dream. Ahead lay pearly sky and great cumulus clouds lit from the west as the sun went down. I went below to fix supper in the galley. By the time we'd finished eating, it was dark with only the ship's running lights and the pink glow of the instrument panel showing until Dale pointed out the red and green lights at the mouth of the harbor.

We awoke in Port Washington to blue sky and swallows in the rigging. Dale sat at the navigation desk walking a compass across a lake chart.

"Frankfurt, Michigan, is one hundred nautical miles away, bearing 45 degrees. If we leave right now, we can be there by midnight." He folded the chart. "It's a beautiful day. We're going sailing my friend! No more of this motoring stuff!"

Clear of the harbor, we attached the big spinnaker to the bowsprit and ran it up, but by then the wind had died and Dale reluctantly switched on the auxiliary motor.

The horizon seemed cut with an Exacto knife, a thin line dividing blue sky from bluer water. At midafternoon, a smudge of coal smoke appeared on the line and grew larger and larger until a red smokestack and black hull appeared beneath it. The USS *Badger* was steaming toward Michigan. When my children were little we took the car ferry to visit relatives, a five-hour crossing that featured an accordion player with a monkey on the outer deck. The trip was considered a great success, and for a long time afterward, the kids turned every large cardboard box into a lake boat. Half a century ago, a Great Lakes cruise was not the sole province of yacht owners and their friends. Twenty overnight passenger vessels once operated between Lake Superior and Lake Ontario, and Midwesterners could enjoy a leisurely cruise without having to fly to Florida and board a hysterical "fun ship."

A fifteen-knot wind came up as the sun went down, so Dale shut off the diesel engine to give us the full effect of night sailing. There was a waning moon and a full complement of stars. Every time a whitecap whooshed past, the boat would lift a little. At the wheel I felt like I was driving at night with the headlights off, the car pointed toward the winking lights of Frankfurt. As we neared the harbor, Dale took the wheel. That night I revisited Captain Slocum: "There was no wind at all, and the sea became smooth and monotonous."

Two days later we waited in a cold drizzle at the Charlevoix drawbridge before beginning the final leg of the trip. Behind us was a J-35, a predecessor to the J-109 but not as fast, according to Dale.

"Where are you headed?" shouted the man at the older boat's helm.

"Mackinac Island," said Dale.

"Us too."

The drawbridge rose and we broke into the lake chop, but while we paused to raise the mainsail, the J-35 slipped ahead of us.

"We're not in a race," said Dale.

Maybe he was worried about a scarcity of slips at Mackinac Island, or perhaps he was just being competitive, but we steadily gained on the J-35 before overtaking her near the lighthouse at Ile Aux Galets. Then we began our southern approach to the Straits of Mackinac through an area of shoals by lining up with Gray's Reef Light Station, a bleak square of concrete, unmanned except for flocks of black cormorants. Dale had a sentimental attachment to the lighthouse because it's a pivotal point in the Chicago to Mackinac Race and many racers have had their ashes spread there. As we slowed to throw chocolate-chip cookies in the water in remembrance of all those departed sailors, the J-35 took a shortcut through the shoals.

"We're not in a race," Dale repeated, standing at the wheel in the storm light, his jaw set in a determined line. "But if the wind holds, we'll catch them at the bridge."

A stiff west wind heeled *Zig-Zag* over until we were sailing full and bye. Then the puff vanished as quickly as it had come, and we watched the J-35 pass beneath the great suspension bridge and turn south into Lake Huron.

As it turned out, there were plenty of available slips on Mackinac Island that afternoon. We were tying up when a pair of elderly women in tweed outfits and hats marched down the dock. The taller one resembled Miss Marple.

"Have you raced this J-boat?" she asked.

"I have," said Dale. He must have recognized something in the old woman's manner because he asked if she sailed.

"Not anymore. I'm eighty years old," she said, smiling a little. "But I did race on Chesapeake Bay. I belonged to the Baltimore Yacht Club, and we sailed every Wednesday and Saturday night."

"Do you miss it?"

"Oh yes," she said. "Or I wouldn't be talking to you."

Summer Night

THE SUN HAS GONE DOWN and with it the heat. At the other end of the farm, the moon has yet to rise, though enough light remains to see dark rows of raspberry bushes and a pale field road climbing into a darker forest of corn. Dusk is being replaced by something else: the flickering bioluminescence of fireflies. This summer's heat coupled with last summer's rains have produced a bumper crop of lightning bugs, all flashing intermittently. These winking green lights act as a sexual beacon to other fireflies. The males flash and glow and the females flash back. Even a bystander can sense the night fill with yearning.

We're sitting around a small fire at the edge of the raspberry patch waiting for the moon to rise. It's early August and already the end of raspberry season. In a week or so, there will be the creaking of crickets instead of this heavy stillness. You can almost feel summer poised to begin its steady descent into autumn, as if tonight were a fulcrum that could tilt either way.

My wife and her sister planted early varieties—Killarneys, Novas, and Jewels—on an acre of what had been an alfalfa field. They mulched the slender raspberry canes with woodchips, planted clover between the rows, and trellised the thorny branches by stringing wire between T-posts. They hired pickers and conscripted spouses. They bought a commercial refrigerator for the barn to keep the fragile berries cool until they could be sold by the pint to groceries and farmer's markets.

An acre of raspberries is a lot to pick. It's the equivalent of a football field minus the end zones. On hot days I'd finish a one-hundred-yard row, then start over again to find the unpicked berries already softening. It was a race against ripeness. It was also a race against picnic beetles, fruit worms, and the spotted-wing *Drosophilia*, a fruit fly that lays its eggs in overripe berries and turns them to a maggoty pulp. The taste of raspberries must be woven into the DNA of even the simplest organism along with an innate understanding of summer as something sweet that's over too soon.

After more than a century, the farm itself is up in the air—some siblings want to take their inheritance in money and others in land—and while the family debated whether to sell, my wife and her sister did, on a small scale, what previous generations had always done: made the land pay. Tonight we're celebrating the end of their first raspberry season, not knowing whether there will be another. Every face within the campfire's glow belongs to someone I've known the better part of my life. I'd tell them how much they mean to me except it would spoil the mood, so I crack another beer instead.

A brother-in-law shouts and we all look up to see a nearly full moon float above the cornfield. Something in that muted light, the way the moon has turned the tasseled field a deep blue-gray, reminds me of a painting I'd seen years ago in an Edvard Munch exhibition. Not as edgy or well known as *The Scream,* Munch's *Summer Night's Dream* falls on the opposite end of the emotional scale. A young woman in a white dress stands in a grove of trees, backlit by just such a shaft of yellow light. The woman stares off the canvas, arms behind her back, face inclined forward, her features blurred not only by the dim moonlight but by her own intense yearning. Every part of her body is held in check except her eyes, which are wide open. What is she looking at? Her lover, perhaps. Or maybe she's just lost in the evening itself, in the ineffable beauty of the moment, knowing it won't last.

That's how I feel on this summer night—as if nothing else matters, not tomorrow or the next day or whatever lies beyond. Sometimes it's enough to hold tight to the moment, to sit unblinking in the glow of things, your heart swollen with so many emotions that if you opened your mouth to explain you couldn't be sure what might come out.

Family Reunion

EVERY SUMMER Uncle Frank and Aunt Marcella invited us to their cottage on Delavan Lake for a family reunion. This was my late father's side of the family. I was only seven when he died, and for many years afterwards my mother made a point of driving all day to attend these gatherings so we'd get to know his brothers and sisters. Otherwise we hardly ever saw them.

The layout of the reunion was always the same: concentric rings of relatives arranged by age and radiating outward from the lake. The children spent all day swimming or wading and left the water only when called to eat. My aunts, who'd prepared the corn on the cob and potato salad and hamburgers, sat in folding chairs on the shore, legs crossed, smoking cigarettes and holding babies. Farther up the lawn, their husbands pitched horseshoes and drank beer.

Uncles fascinated me. Like Darwin's finches, they were variations on a theme. They all spoke in flat Chicago accents, complaining that the weather was terribly "hat" or grumbling about traffic on the toll road to "Wiss-**kan**-sin." Whenever one dispensed a somber pronouncement, the others would nod in unison. My favorite was Uncle Richard, my father's youngest brother, a big-boned, heavy-jawed man who possessed the sort of physique associated with Soviet-era monuments to The Worker. Sufficiently cajoled, he'd allow himself to be used as a human catapult for flinging us into the lake. Finally, far up the long green slope was the family's point of origin, my paternal grandparents, who sat in the shadow of a giant Norway pine and hardly moved.

These get-togethers at the lake continued unabated for years, though my interest in them waned as I got older and stopped altogether once I got my driver's license. By that time I couldn't see wasting a precious summer weekend on relatives.

Which was a shame.

Like weddings and funerals, a family reunion offers a vantage point from which past and future can be glimpsed simultaneously. As a skinny kid, I could look at Uncle Richard's musculature and find cause for hope. Similarly, when my uncles horsed around at the lake, I could recognize myself as they briefly reverted to being someone's little boys, someone else's goofy brothers. And what I wouldn't give now to go back and quiz my grandparents—*What was it like growing up at the tail end of the nineteenth century? Was life better when there were fewer cars and more horses?* But children live so completely in the present they can't imagine a world that isn't fixed and unchanging.

I was married with a child of my own before I attended another family reunion at Delavan Lake. Instead of driving up from Chicago, we came down from the north, so there was none of the old magic of "going to Wisconsin." The driveway still curved through oak woods but now led to a new cottage, the original having burned down after a lightning strike. Everything else was the same, except the cast of characters had been reshuffled. I no longer recognized the kids splashing in the lake, and the men now played volleyball instead of horseshoes. My grandparents were long gone, their place beneath the great Norway pine taken by white-haired aunts and uncles who sat in the shade toward which we were all slowly progressing.

Uncle Richard was there, though no longer the colossus of my youth. It seemed strange to sit with him drinking beer as more or less an equal. I'd heard he'd weathered some tough times, divorce and career setbacks, but we didn't talk about current events. Instead we talked about people no longer present. Parenthood had begun to make me wonder about my own family origins as if the past might illuminate what came next. So I asked Uncle Richard what he remembered of his older brother. He paused a moment to unreel the years.

"Your father," he said, "was a peach of a man."

SEPTEMBER

Migrations

FOR SEVERAL YEARS the first week in September meant a long car ride south down the interstate in a van loaded with bedding, a laptop, a new suitcase, and a child who wouldn't be returning until Thanksgiving. Across the median strip, other vans and cars with rooftop carriers would be streaming north, all part of a great seasonal migration between home and campus. At rest stops and fast-food joints, I'd recognize the parents of other college-bound teenagers by their grim cheerfulness and air of preoccupation. They'd look at their wristwatches, check tie-downs, steal glances at the departing child. Behind the brave smiles, they shared a single worry: what if my son or daughter returns in a few months aloof and estranged to sit, as essayist Richard Rodriguez once put it, "like an anthropologist at the kitchen table?"

I never lost sleep over this question for two reasons. First, I teach at a university and understand that higher education is *meant* to make the familiar seem strange in the same way that travel does. The second reason is that there was always another child waiting at the kitchen table when we got home. This time is different because we're dropping off our last child and the house we'll return to won't be empty exactly, but awfully, awfully quiet, and that will be strange indeed.

In previous Septembers the road to college followed I-94 to Madison, the countryside whipping past at sixty-five miles per hour. This time we're driving to UW–La Crosse on a two-lane through the Driftless Area, a slow road that winds through hills and coulee towns with old brick facades. When the kids were little we made frequent forays from home on roads just like this one, meandering trips to cranberry marshes at harvest time or limestone caverns in the summer dog days or tours of old lead mines or historic sites led by elderly docents who seemed to be recalling their own childhoods. There were visits to art museums and county fairs and powwows where the whole sky throbbed with drumbeats, excursions to dry-docked submarines and petting zoos and weird concrete sculptures made of seashells and tie-rods and old beer bottles. We considered all these trips educational in the sense that they were intended to provoke a sense of wonder as well as belonging, as if to assure the children, "What an *interesting* place you live in!"

During his college career my son will doubtless encounter some version of Professor Marvel ("Professor Marvel never guesses! He knows!"), the sort of academic so keen to defamiliarize students from their own experiences that they end up believing the wide world begins in some distant place—New York or London or wherever Professor Marvel went to graduate school. It's fine to want students to be at home in the world, but first they have to feel at home.

I remember another, much shorter journey on my son's first day of formal education. The three-block walk from home to preschool took forever that morning not because the boy was apprehensive, except about the looming prospect of naps, but because he was so absorbed by everything along the way. Every few steps he'd stoop to examine some new wonder—a fallen leaf, cracks in the sidewalk, a line of ants on the march—as if everything was worthy of attention. I'm afraid I played the role of Professor Marvel that day, dragging the little fellow by the arm, hurrying him along so we'd get there on time. "We're here," I announced at the school door, then left him to face the alphabet and naptime alone.

Now our positions are reversed. Fixed on the future, that cloud-land of possibility, he's eager to get to the dorm on time, while I wish our ride could go on forever. When we get there, things will be rushed and awkward and I'll forget what I want to tell him, which is this: Trust your instincts. What feels worthwhile and true now shouldn't change overnight. And if home seems a little strange come Thanksgiving, it's because you never had to think of *home* as an idea before—as a choice—and now you do. But that's okay. Take your time. We're not going anywhere.

Farm Beginnings

AT DUSK on a recent fall weekend I sat down to a potluck supper in a converted calf barn on a farm near Osceola. The barn doors were open at either end, and between the hot dishes and homemade pie I watched a pair of border collies intently herding small children through the yard's golden light. It was the sort of animals-and-children scene reproduced on a thousand calendars that makes farming seem like a rural idyll instead of a tough business.

That notion of farming as part of the good life has steadily lost ground over the last several decades to a harsher view, the economics of scale, by which American farmers have been repeatedly told to "get big or get out." Many took that advice and got out. At the turn of the last century, about the time my hosts' upright-and-wing farmhouse was built, nearly half the country's population was engaged in agriculture. Now it's fewer than 2 percent. The cost of this demographic shift can be measured in empty farmsteads and in the gutted small towns that once served them. Or you can simply stand outside at sunset and watch the near total darkness come over the countryside at night.

The most recent US Census of Agriculture, however, reveals a surprising change. For the first time in seventy years, the number of farms in the country actually increased. Most of that increase was in small farms run by young operators who produce something other than corn, soybeans, and grain-fed beef. The dozen or so people attending the potluck supper in the barn that night represent this new demographic. They are recent graduates of a program called Farm Beginnings. The ten-month course run by the Land Stewardship Project is designed to help newcomers break into agriculture and provide established farmers with an alternative to the endless cycle of larger fields, bigger machinery, and debt.

Before supper our hosts Jen and Lorin Demulling led a walking tour of their farm. Three generations of Demullings had run it as a dairy operation when Lorin began milking full time out of high school. He told me, "Half the kids in my class farmed back then. Now I think there's one left." The exodus from farming was often the result of one person trying to do what had previously occupied an entire family. After his father retired, Lorin was milking sixty to seventy cows twice a day as well as doing cash crops and working himself to exhaustion. In the end, he sold the herd and took a job in town.

The farm still looks like a traditional dairy operation—three silos, a pond, and a granary—except for the lack of Holsteins. The cows have been replaced by long rows of strawberries and asparagus and a large vegetable garden. Lorin and Jen began the switch to a CSA (community-supported agriculture) because they wanted to raise their children on the farm. While Farm Beginnings offers classroom instruction and field trips, what the Demullings found most useful was the network of other farmers they could call upon for advice and support.

One reason farming is a difficult business is that it's done in isolation. Unlike their contemporaries in the European Union, American farmers don't dump their produce in the streets or take to the barricades when squeezed by market forces. Instead, when the end comes, they go down quietly with the ship, one ship at a time. Programs like Farm Beginnings lessen the sense of isolation by providing a different sort of rural neighborhood, one in which cell phones and the Internet connect neighbors instead of fence lines.

"Our goal is for the farm to be self-sustaining," said Lorin. "The community has been quite accepting. The market is there. You just have to go out and establish it."

Since this was a commencement ceremony of sorts, after supper the graduates were asked to share the challenges they'd faced in their new ventures as well as the rewards. One burly fellow described the difficulty of convincing his father to switch their cows from corn to grass. For most participants, the challenges of small-scale farming were hardly distinguishable from the rewards.

By evening the last remnants of golden light had drained out of the sky and onto the surface of the Demullings' pond, against which the outbuildings were silhouetted. Amy Bacigalupo, director of the Land Stewardship Project, talked about how nights had grown blacker on her own family farm over the years as the windows of one neighbor's place after another went dark. She hoped that trend could be reversed. Then she handed a lit candle to each of the graduates until the whole barn was flickering with light.

Poultry

THE TROUBLE BEGAN when some of my neighbors asked city officials to legalize what they had quietly been doing all along— raising a few hens in backyard coops. Weary of guerilla farming, they wanted the freedom to raise their chickens in broad daylight. The benefits seemed obvious. Chickens convert milled corn into fresh eggs and garden fertilizer while providing their owners with colorful and amusing pets. A proposal was drafted to limit city residents to no more than five hens, zero roosters, and to prohibit selling eggs or slaughtering chickens. But the idea of "urban chickens" struck a nerve with some city council members, and by the time the measure reached a vote its implications had swelled under the weight of opposing narratives.

Many of the pro-chicken crowd, henceforth referred to as the AGENTS OF CHANGE, work at the same university I do, and they're good people, conscientious and sincere to a fault though they tend to overconceptualize even simple things, which is why department meetings can last for days and days. Their narrative skipped over the more obvious reasons for raising poultry, like money or just for the hell of it, and soared into more ethereal issues. Raising backyard chickens wasn't just about the eggs. It was about a healthy lifestyle. It was about serving your family protein incubated beside the backyard swing set rather than on a factory farm. Finally, it was about the very future of our city, a city on the cusp of becoming a more aware, much hipper place than it used to be, a place with Internet cafes, a farmers' market, even an alternative newspaper. Backyard coops are part of this bright new future because really hip, vibrant cities like Madison, Chicago, New York, and San Francisco have urban chickens. So why not us? It didn't help that the AGENTS OF CHANGE used words like *progressive* and *sustainability* and *environmental,* words almost never found in poultry catalogues.

In contrast, the anti-chicken narrative put forward by the FORCES OF REACTION could be reduced to one simple but compelling idea. That idea was NO! Not in my neighbor's backyard. No way. If you allow chickens in the city, could pigs and goats and Spanish fighting bulls be far behind? This Domino Theory was coupled with dire warnings about public health. Chickens may look colorful and fun, but any farm boy knows they're magnets for vermin and pestilence; raising one in your backyard would be the equivalent of inviting a pimp to dinner. Country people know this, which is why so many have moved to the city—to escape chickens.

A city council member with direct poultry experience echoed the narrator of Sherwood Anderson's story "The Egg," who confesses that if "I am a gloomy man inclined to see the darker side of life, I attribute it to the fact that what should have been for me the happy joyous days of childhood were spent on a chicken farm." This sentiment carried the day, as the city council voted 8–3 against the proposal.

As someone without a horse (or chicken) in this particular race, I could see that the controversy was as much about what constitutes city life as it was about poultry. People who grow up in the country tend to categorize animals strictly by use and dislike ambiguity, like confusing a barn cat with a house cat; city people, on the other hand, view any creature as a potential pet. The urban chicken proposal had aroused these opposing sensibilities so that both sides missed the other's points. As one city councilman declared, "people have come here to live in a city, and chickens is pretty unexpected in a city."

Yes they is.

One sympathetic voice on the council suggested the AGENTS OF CHANGE needed to do a better job "educating the public" about the nature of chickens. Allow me to try by sharing a little story.

My mother-in-law used to keep a flock of white leghorns on the farm and sold the eggs to a local grocers for pocket money until laws requiring egg inspection compelled them to buy only from large producers whose chickens were raised in battery cages instead of on the ground. In her later years she kept a dozen layers for family use. During our visits to the farm she'd send our oldest daughter to collect the eggs, hoping in the process the girl would absorb some of the ethos of farm work. The air inside the coop would be stuffy and swirling with dust motes and the conspiratorial murmurings of white leghorns. Most of the hens nested in their boxes, but others milled about the floor, a thick mat of feathers, straw, and curdled droppings. The chickens looked more reptilian than fowl, with their small, reddish eyes and leathery wattles. When our ten-year-old reached gingerly for an egg, the hen sitting on it suddenly squawked. She jerked her hand away, dropping the egg on the floor. Instantly, all the hens swarmed to the glistening orange yolk and began pecking at it. The girl was horrified, yes, but also fascinated by this unexpected turn of events, so much more complicated—and interesting—than the simple fictions she'd been told about chickens. Pulling another egg from the nest, she held it suspended over the floor until she had the hens' attention. Then slowly, deliberately, she let it drop.

Looking for Trouble

WHAT REMAINS MEMORABLE after a journey are the things that went wrong. The capsized boat, the detour to nowhere, that little supper at the nightmare café—all these mishaps gain in reflection because they can be put into a story. And it's the story that you remember. The perfect vacation fades over time because there's no narrative to lovely sunsets or waiters who aren't surly. Misfortune, on the other hand, has a way of making the world feel strange and new, and isn't that the point of travel? Forget where you're going, says the blown tire. Look where you are!

When I was young and car-less, I enjoyed hitchhiking for the randomness it brought to travel. Thumbing from Daytona Beach to Fort Lauderdale one spring break to visit a girl, I had a close call when someone in a screaming white convertible filled with people my age hurled a sixty-mile-per-hour grapefruit at me. It missed. But here's the point: I can no longer recall the face of the girl I was hitchhiking to see, a young woman I thought I loved. Now all I remember is the yellow arc of grapefruit as it sailed past palmetto trees and smashed into the pavement at my feet as if to say "Welcome to Florida!" Over time I've come to recognize the hurled grapefruit for what it was: an unexpected gift.

Tourism—paying X amount of dollars for X amount of fun— serves to isolate the traveler from locals and make it harder to distinguish acts of kindness from contractual obligations. The well-heeled tourist is constantly digging into his pocket to tip the natives for singing "Hooray for Captain Spaulding!" But anyone who's ever stopped to ask directions knows that the best way to ingratiate yourself with locals is to show incompetence.

On a motorcycle trip through Nova Scotia, I found myself marooned at an isolated crossroads. All day I'd been riding toward the coast only to have my engine conk out at this little gas station in the middle of nowhere. Now it was dark and beginning to rain. Mechanics and assorted loafers filed out of the station and watched me try the starter. Nothing. Then they each took a turn. Too bad, they said, then told me their life stories. Roaring into the station an hour earlier, I'd been of no interest, but once I was transformed into a Man of Misfortune the locals couldn't do enough for me. One fellow put me up for the night at the house he shared with his fiancée. Another loaded my lifeless bike into the back of his pickup the next morning and drove me to a repair shop in Halifax. (The problem was a cracked coil.) When I offered gas money or breakfast, my benefactor refused. He'd seen *me* as the problem, and once I'd been solved he saw no reason to reverse our roles. Later that day I reached the coast, which was beautiful in ways I no longer remember.

Now that I'm the one planning family trips, I do my best to limit randomness. I make lists, study the map, keep an eye on the weather. On a recent trip to Door County, we rode mountain bikes on a trail through the woods until they opened to a lovely campsite on Duck Bay. We pitched our tent and cooked supper over a campfire. After the day's heat, the cool breeze off the bay came as a welcome relief. Later that night I awoke to a premonitory rumbling. Thunder boomed in the distance, then grew louder until the storm sounded like it was stomping down the stairs in a bad mood. The walls bellowed in and out from the wind, and I realized I hadn't staked down the tent. Imagining us parasailing into the night, I stretched my body the length of the tent, arms and legs splayed to anchor the corners. The gravity of the situation escaped my wife. Between lightning flashes, she amused the children by telling them that Gumby was having a nightmare.

Next morning, a new tributary flowed under the tent floor toward Lake Michigan. Our sleeping bags had become islands. Everything was soaking wet. Afterward, we all agreed it was the best part of the trip.

OCTOBER

Gridiron

OUR FIRST APARTMENT was a bleak walk-up a few blocks from the stadium where, on alternating Friday nights during the fall, the city's high schools gathered to play football. On warm evenings, I could hear the games through our kitchen window. I'd follow the play-by-play, not so much the announcer's words garbled over the loudspeaker as his manic intonation whenever someone galloped into the end zone. Each touchdown was followed with a great exhalation and then a lesser one, like an echo, when the new score was confirmed. Halftime announced itself with the thud of tom-toms, snare and bass drums vibrating through the autumn air as a marching band erupted into "In-A-Gadda-Da-Vida" or "Louie, Louie" or some other rock standard transformed into something playable on a tuba to a four-four beat.

For big games between crosstown rivals, people would start parking in front of our apartment half an hour before kickoff and walk to the stadium. Some nights my wife and I would join them, the long procession of fans strung along both sides of the street carrying blankets and wearing school colors. Because the stadium occupies the high ground of a city park, we could look above the dark trees to see the night sky haloed above the field like the glow of a great city. Once inside, there was the strange excitement of reversal—of night turned into day, children allowed up past bedtimes, one's own voice caught up in the whirlwind of the crowd.

I didn't care which teams played or who won. I loved being part of the game, not just the action between the hash marks but the whole surrounding spectacle. Small-town football is the great autumnal drama, an Everyman play in four acts with its own stock characters and subplots: the assistant coach smacking a kid on the helmet for a blown play, reserves in spotless uniforms screaming red faced on the sidelines, flirtations and intrigues behind the stands, small fry tossing a football around the end zone at halftime and imagining the future. A few of last year's graduates show up late in their old letter jackets only to leave early because everything has changed. But nothing has changed about the game except their part in it.

People who dismiss high school football because it's not the NFL miss the point, or else their memories of it are still too painful. In high school, everyone is assigned a role—jock or nerd or flirt or wallflower—and to say that some people were uncomfortable in their role is a great understatement. To a teenager, there is only Time Present, along with the grim conviction that high school lasts forever.

Football coaches are big on connecting football to life's lessons, like "No pain, no gain" or "Winning isn't everything. It's the only thing." But scoring a touchdown while the whole town cheers isn't necessarily good preparation for whatever comes next. American literature is filled with cautionary tales—John Updike's Rabbit Angstrom novels and Irwin Shaw's story "The Eighty-Yard Run"—of men who remained boys by believing such simple maxims. Better to spend Friday nights high-stepping across the field in a maroon cape while playing the clarinet for the sheer love of playing it even as the crowd recedes toward the concession stands. That's more like what comes next.

If small-town football teaches anything, it's the circularity of life. The same characters may show up for the big game year after year, but the parts are always recast. Soon enough, yesterday's gridiron hero shares the stands with the ex-clarinet player, both of them cheering on their former selves.

Lifeboat

THE OVERLAP between summer's end and the onset of fall complicates even the simplest things, like getting dressed. If I wear a jacket to work in the morning, it'll ride home on my shoulder at the end of the day. Or I'll drive to a Friday night football game even as the metronomic voice of Bob Uecker is calling a doubleheader on the radio. It's disorienting. In early October I'm still doing the arithmetic on my summer wish list, toting up the fun things that I did or didn't do, like catch a fish or swim in both freshwater and a chlorinated pool. I try not to think about autumn's list because that one's all chores.

Fall is the kingdom of Austerity, a somber place where lackadaisical grasshoppers must transform themselves into busy ants while the sun still shines. But it's hard to when the weather remains perfect for fiddling around. Who wants to pack away the lawn chairs and badminton net and charcoal grill when to do so would mean admitting that summer is over, really over, kaput?

Most of fall is just preparation for winter, anyway. I don't mind getting the house ready—putting up storm windows, laying in firewood, caulking and glazing—all of which makes the house sound like an iron-hulled ship I'm battening down for a long Arctic voyage. Or maybe I just like language that makes dull chores sound exciting and purposeful, like saying "storm windows" instead of "secondary sashes."

The garden is a different story. Putting the garden to bed for the year is one sad goodbye after another. After working at half speed all summer, the garden is just hitting its stride, pumping out so many tomatoes and zucchini that you take to piling them on the coffee-room table at work with little signs that read: FREE TO GOOD HOME or ARE YOU MY MOTHER? It's as if the plants know something terrible is on the horizon and are making a last ditch effort to ingratiate themselves.

According to the US Department of Agriculture, our backyard garden falls within Plant Hardiness Zone 4, the same as Billings, Montana, with an average growing season of 145 days. The season ends with the first frost around the autumnal equinox, give or take a day. There are premonitory warnings—the arrival of a solid gray cloudbank, big as an iceberg and sailing in on a brisk northerly wind. These signs are later confirmed by the weatherman on the ten o'clock news, who points to the approaching frontal boundary with abrupt, antlike gestures.

The next few nights we're out with flashlights and old bed sheets to cover the tomatoes, basil, and less-hardy flowers. In the morning, the garden looks de-masted. We pick and freeze as many vegetables as possible to save them from, well, freezing. We eat a lot of pesto and ratatouille—so much ratatouille that I begin to resent eggplant, especially the small ones that will never amount to anything. And whose idea was it to plant so many bell peppers in the first place?

After three nights of flashlights and sheets, the gardener makes the final call. "Oh, to hell with it!"

The garden's final evening is starlit and strangely becalmed. Our breaths appear in the flashlight beams as quick puffs of smoke. Without a word, we carry potted plants into the house. This is the brutal truth of gardening: in the end, some plants get a seat in the lifeboat; the others are set adrift. So farewell broccoli and Roma tomatoes! Good-bye basil and Bibb lettuce. It's been sweet knowing you these few short months, but here is where our paths diverge. Now I'm going inside a warm, well-lighted house and closing the door while you remain outside to freeze in the dark. I'll remember you every night in my dreams, especially the fresh salads, but my heart will go on.

Library

IN MY HOMETOWN, three buildings offered portholes through which a child might glimpse the adult world: the movie theater, the church, and the public library. Each was an imposing structure whose spacious interior provoked silence as well as a certain dreaminess. In the first two, the dreaminess lasted only as long as the homily or double feature. But a trip to the library could set off dreaminess that lasted a lifetime.

Our public library had a bright, airy new children's addition, which I avoided, preferring the more somber adult section with its churchlike hush and dark warren of old bookshelves that seemed like the Fort Knox of Knowledge. Every subject a twelve-year-old could possibly find interesting was shelved in those aisles: deep-sea fishing, tombs of the Pharaohs, medieval heraldry, survival techniques. All one needed was a library card and a basic grasp of the Dewey Decimal System. After trancelike hours imaging myself battling marlin in the Gulf Stream and surviving the ensuing shipwreck, I'd thump a pyramid of books in front of the checkout librarian, whose cat-eye glasses hung from a chain around her neck.

Today the Internet is the Fort Knox of Knowledge. Children are more likely to look for the world by peering into a computer screen than at the pages of a book. The typical library patron now checks out seven books a year, half as many as thirty years ago, but makes up the difference in CDs, DVDs, and video tapes. Public libraries provide everything from Internet access to tax forms, but few of them resemble the quiet refuge I remember from childhood.

One that still does is the Bayfield public library. Built in 1903 on a hillside overlooking Lake Superior, it's a Greek Revival shoebox with a columned portico of locally quarried brownstone. Inside, it manages to feel both austere and cozy. There are fireplaces at either end, a vaulted ceiling, and tall windows that flood the room with lake light. It feels like a rich man's study—which, in a manner of speaking, it is.

The Bayfield library is one of 1,689 public libraries built across the United States between 1883 and 1929 by steel tycoon Andrew Carnegie. Many were constructed in small towns that could not afford a grand public building, let alone the books to fill one. Of the sixty-three Carnegie libraries built in Wisconsin, two-thirds have been demolished or else converted to B&Bs or private homes. Those remaining in operation are easy to recognize even without the benefactor's name carved into the lintel because Carnegie's private secretary established their basic blueprint. In "Notes on Library Building," James Bertram called for "a plain, dignified structure" of one story, rectangular in shape, with separate reading rooms for adults and children and space in the basement for a public lecture room, toilets, and a boiler. That's the Bayfield library in a nutshell, except for the computers tucked into side rooms.

Andrew Carnegie's framed portrait still hangs above one of the fireplaces in the Bayfield library. It's the same portrait that was donated to every Carnegie library in 1935, the centennial of the great philanthropist's birth. The picture shows the wee Scotsman holding a book even as he levels a pair of wistful blue eyes at the viewer. A former bobbin boy in a textile mill, Carnegie offered himself as proof of the American Dream, a wage slave who rose to become the richest man in the world. He was also a robber baron and strikebreaker who cut wages at his steel mills even as he donated his surplus wealth to build libraries so that the working poor might improve themselves. In *The Gospel of Wealth*, Carnegie argued that the rich had a moral obligation to improve their communities by donating to schools and libraries so that "the industrious and ambitious" might better themselves. How they were to find time for self-improvement after working a twelve-hour day he didn't say. A few cities with strong labor unions debated whether to accept Carnegie's charity, arguing that the millionaire was only building monuments to himself. But in the end they took the money. Who says no to a library?

Libraries, even old ones like Bayfield's, are always about the future. From his own experience, Carnegie knew that some daydreams begun among the bookshelves sooner or later turn into deeds. He trusted that posterity would remember his good deeds rather than his business methods. And so it has—even if the schoolchildren trooping downstairs for afternoon storytime haven't the slightest idea who the bearded old man in the picture is.

Wonderland

MY DATE AND I were walking back to her dorm after a movie, a comedy, I think. The transition from wide-screen Technicolor to the pale streetlights along Wisconsin Avenue was so abrupt that for a moment I forgot it was fall and that I was living in a city for the first time. Passing Gesu Church, its massive twin towers disappearing into the darkness, we ducked into the shadow of a gothic doorway, and there in the dim recesses I bent to kiss the girl's face. Sadly, it's a face I can no longer recall, only the horse laugh that had issued from it earlier at the movie. The girl returned my kiss, so we were briefly, in the parlance of the time, making out.

Somebody shouted above the wash of traffic. I raised my head to see a figure all in black—black overcoat, black fedora, black pants, and black shoes—rushing toward us. Then I saw the glint of a white Roman collar. The man was a priest, and his face was livid.

"Get away from there!" he shouted. "What do you think you're doing? You ought to be ashamed!"

Suddenly I *was* ashamed—blood rising to my face, my ears burning—because a large man was yelling at me in front of my date. I hoped he'd simply go away, but the priest stood his ground, then slowly extended an arm like a flaming sword and pointed us toward the street. We walked back to the dorm in silence. I never saw the girl again.

Any number of themes might be drawn from such a story—a fall from grace, the tensions of celibacy, carnal youth—but what strikes me now, after all these years, is my lack of respect for a great building.

A city is its buildings. As a lonely college freshman, I'd wandered Milwaukee every weekend with my eyes at street level looking for girls, not the city's architectural treasures. Gesu Church was a good example of what I'd failed to notice. Henry C. Koch, the architect responsible for City Hall and the Pfister Hotel, had designed Gesu as a miniature Chartres, from the uneven square towers to the great rose window at the gable end. I had a personal history with that church, having attended my uncle's ordination to the priesthood there in the mid-1950s. It was a ponderously long ceremony in Latin, but I certainly would have been awed by the soaring architecture in the same way I was awed by hotel elevators and civic statuary, all part of the giddy new experience of being in a city. Ushered inside those gothic doors, I would have confronted the totally unexpected space between the floor of the nave and its vaulted ceiling, the echo of people shuffling into pews, the altar candles burning at the apsidal end.

Of course, it helps now to know the language of architecture, but even a child unequipped to name the parts of the church can appreciate their cumulative effect—which is amazement. Too often there's a tendency to equate our experience in a great building with our experience in nature, for example comparing the lofty supporting columns of a nave with a grove in a forest. But a "cathedral of the pines" is always a happy accident, while the awe we feel in a cathedral is deliberate, a direct result of the architect's vision. And this sense of wonder isn't limited to churches or old buildings. One feels it in the Milwaukee Art Museum's Quadracci Pavillion, designed by Santiago Calatrava, its expansive white marble floor and winglike ceiling as if the building stood poised to take flight.

I remain a churchgoer by temperament as well as training. Occasionally during a dull homily my mind will wander from the pulpit to the babies draped over their parents' shoulders in pews ahead of me. What could they possibly make of the service, I wonder, these small, backward-facing parishioners? When not making goo-goo eyes at me, they seem otherwise enthralled with the experience of the building: its great vault of air above their heads, the prism of stained glass, those revolving ceiling fans—*What are they?*—and the echoing acoustics, which they test with sudden yelps and loud jabbering like tiny singers running the scales.

NOVEMBER

Firewood

SATURDAY. A perfect early November morning—sunlight tunneling beneath a gunmetal sky—except for the sliding sensation of being between seasons. One night soon I'll go to bed in autumn and wake up to winter's chill. Toward that inevitability, I'm crunching gravel on Skinner Creek Road, driving slow enough to make any game warden take notice except that I'm not hunting deer but firewood.

The road loops through a forest of northern hardwoods zebra striped with white birch. October's brilliant confetti-fall of leaves has been replaced by bare treetops and sky. Despite the wildlife—already I've seen a large gray doe and a shaggy brown bobcat cross the road—this is a working forest. Logging roads angle off on either side, some overgrown, others freshly gated. What I'm looking for is the slash-and-tangle of last year's logging so I can scavenge the remains. A permit on my dashboard entitles me to cut a staggering ten pulp cords (the equivalent of twenty-five face cords) of dead and downed trees from Price County forests. The number of permits issued has risen steadily along with the cost of fuel oil. Cutting their own firewood might be an act of self-sufficiency for most people; for me it's escapism, since I only have to heat a weekend cabin through the winter.

The first thing anyone notices about logging is the damage left behind: the chaotic thicket of raspberry brambles and saplings that replaces a mature stand of aspen after a clear-cut. The violence looks indiscriminate, but often it's a case of our not seeing the forest for the trees. My cabin neighbor, Roy Gilge, is a timber cruiser for the state forest, and when he goes into the woods he's paid to see both. He'll do a "recon" before a timber sale, measuring the diameter of individual trees at chest height to calculate their "basal area," and then add those figures together to arrive at a group portrait of the hardwood stand. He'll mark trees to be cut with a slash of orange paint, a dot above the slash if the tree contains saw logs, and leave the rest as "crop trees." Maple and white ash require shade to grow, so hardwood stands are periodically thinned rather than leveled. Aspen, on the other hand, grows best in open sunlight, so it's clear-cut on a forty- to forty-five-year rotation, close to the tree's natural lifespan. The result is a forest with an uneven silhouette, one less aesthetically pleasing than a climax forest entirely of hardwoods, but probably more diverse in wildlife. While some species—pine marten and migrant songbirds like the scarlet tanager—require old growth, others such as deer, grouse, and woodcock do better in young forests. The ideal forest would be one big enough to hold tracts of both.

The road corkscrews down a hill, through an alder swamp and parts of two townships, before coming to a hardwood ridge, where I park the van. The recently thinned stand looks parklike aside from the cut boughs and tops I intend to convert into BTUs. White ash is my first preference, followed by hard maple and finally white birch, which doesn't burn as long but ignites quickly and looks pretty in a woodbox. After the pinging car ride, the forest is overwhelmingly quiet—at least until I rev up the chainsaw. Then it sounds like a motocross track. The noise doesn't seem to bother a chickadee flitting overhead as I saw a toppled maple into six-foot lengths. Drying on the ground for a year, the log has lost nearly half its live weight—though "skidding" it to the van on my shoulder is still an effort.

Sunday. I buck the logs into stove-length pieces beside the cabin, then use a neighbor's hydraulic log-splitter to cleave each piece into quarters. In years past I've used an eight-pound maul, which was more picturesque but brutally inaccurate when it came to splitting small-diameter logs. I prefer the machine's inexhaustible efficiency and the way it produces perfect, wedge-shaped pieces, the smooth white grain of the wood showing against the bark. In an hour I've got a pyramid of firewood to stack for next winter's use.

The not-so-distant future. On some freezing afternoon when I've driven two hours to get here, I'll stomp the snow from my boots and drop an armload of firewood into an old crate beside the woodstove. Then I'll lay the fire, building a kind of tunnel with two large logs and filling it with crumpled newspaper and kindling and maybe some strips of birch bark. I'll roof it over with smaller logs and light a match. Once the fire starts to draw, I'll close the stove door and watch through the glass as small chunks of the forest burst into flame to heat my cabin through the night.

The Hunter

IN FAIRY TALES, the hunter is a hero—resourceful, protective, and at home in dark woods. Hunting in these stories, wrote psychologist Bruno Bettelheim, "symbolizes a life close to and in accordance with nature, an existence in line with our more primitive being." But in our modern equivalent of fairy tales, the Disney animated movie, animals are the heroes while the hunter has become a cruel oaf. The role reversal reflects a steady decline in hunting over the past three decades as the country has become less rural and more urban. What child today, for instance, aspires to be Gaston rather than the Beast?

A few months ago I drove to Madison for the annual Deer and Turkey Expo at the Alliant Energy Center out by the city's beltline. While the crowd was mostly men, whole families—mom, grandparents, kids—had also made the trip as they might travel to the state fair or a basketball championship, for an outing and a show of solidarity. These are people for whom hunting is more than a sport, it's a part of their identity, expressed in the clothes they wear, the type of art they hang on their walls, and the decals and bumper stickers on their pickups. Almost everyone wore some item of camouflage clothing so that they blended together into the crowd except the few who didn't and stuck out, like myself.

There was a carnival midway atmosphere on the floor of the exhibition hall that was reminiscent of a state fair. Salesmen in six hundred booths were busy hawking all manner of gadgetry—everything from camouflage ATVs equipped with gun boots to motion detector "stealth" cameras and digital feeding stations—

all designed to ensure my success in the field. There were preloaded scent arrowheads ("IT'S ALMOST NOT FAIR") available in ten scents attractive to big game, elevated stands shaped like pillboxes, mineral supplements that promised "a substantial increase in antler growth," and guided hunts for "an awesome trophy at a great value." The roar of the sales pitch was occasionally broken by the strangely amplified sound of turkey calls—a hennish clucking, a cascading gobble.

The small children accompanying their parents through the hall seemed bored by all the technology on display. Youth are the future of hunting, and if the demographics can be believed, the future looks dim. In Wisconsin the state legislature's response to declining hunter recruitment has been to put deer rifles in ever-smaller hands by lowering the age for a gun license from twelve to ten. (Yikes!) If the young aren't interested in hunting, it isn't for lack of guns but because the sport seems meaningless when it's rigged too heavily in the hunter's favor.

What did hold the children's interest at the expo were booths that featured some representation of the Beast. A steady stream of kids stroked the fox and raccoon pelts at the trapping booth; they gaped at the glass cabinet holding the skeleton of a deer with all the bones identified and at the glass-eyed, antlered deer heads ringing the mezzanine. But the most popular attraction was the Wildlife on Wheels exhibit, where, for a fee, a child could have his or her picture taken with a living eight-month-old black bear cub or ten-month-old grizzly bear cub. The children who posed in front of the painted North Woods backdrop looked far more thrilled with this encounter than the bewildered cub squirming in their hands. Few noticed the disclaimer posted above the LIVE

WILDLIFE EXHIBITION booth explaining that the bears had been raised in captivity.

The hunting community feels so besieged from outside, from animal rights and anti-hunting groups, that it's failed to notice the drift from within as the sport becomes more commercialized, relying on technology instead of the outdoor skills it's supposed to bestow. Hunting has little meaning apart from its larger context, which isn't firearms but land. Hunting is primarily a way of seeing land—reading its surface, trying to see the land the way animals do—rather than improved food plots and mineral supplements. That's not hunting, it's farming.

One of my favorite hunting memories is canoeing down the North Fork of the Flambeau with my son in the predawn gloom of opening morning. I'd scouted that section of state forest the week before in a sudden snowstorm that obliterated all tracks, so I had no idea if any game trails were active. But the topography looked promising, a long ridge overlooking a cedar swamp. This wasn't the dark, monolithic woods of fairy tales but a relatively open hardwood forest that sloped down to the river. We set up at either end of the ridge and then waited. Nothing moved all morning, and I had begun to think about relocating when a rifle shot rang out. I walked to the end of the ridge and found my son standing over a buck he'd shot as it headed out of the swamp. I took off my jacket and gloves and field dressed the deer in the cool morning air. Then we each took hold of an antler and skidded the buck downhill to the canoe. We slid the deer between the thwarts and began to paddle upriver. There was no wind, and the smooth reflection of gray sky and pines dissolved and reformed with each paddle stroke. All this seemed like the beginning or end of a very old story.

Politics

NOT LONG AGO, a woman I know (my wife) drove to Madison for the day. The autumn weather being fine, she decided this was as good a time as any to walk to the state capitol, locate our local representative, and chew him out. She passed through a newly installed security checkpoint, which involved a scanner of the kind used in airports, and into the echoing rotunda, then climbed three flights of marble stairs to the legislative offices. She found the representative at his desk in a double-breasted suit festooned with lapel pins. A tall man, he rose to full height and extended his big right hand. He held the hand out for a long time, well beyond the point when it was clear that she wasn't going to shake it. She moved slightly and the hand followed her. When the representative withdrew the hand and sat down, he smiled a little.

The woman began by asking a few basic questions about the nature of representative government, questions that soon evolved into declarative sentences in the form of accusations. Never had she seen the state so divided, the partisanship so rancorous, neighbor against neighbor. She was almost shaking, but her words rang clear and bitter. "You ought to be ashamed!"

The representative, a bland fellow of wide ties and simple pronouncements, smiled through this tongue lashing as if it was no more than a pleasant summer shower. When it was over, he paused as if deep in thought and said, "It's just politics."

What he meant was this: *Dear lady, the divisiveness you decry is the juice that energizes my base, the war cry that fills party coffers, and it is undoubtedly the reason both you and I are here today.*

168

Lately state politics haven't left me energized but exhausted. I used to enjoy election season, the red and blue posters along the roadsides another form of fall colors. Now they seem like gang signs. It's enough to drive a man to poetry. "Things fall apart; the centre cannot hold," William Butler Yeats wrote nearly a century ago as Europe unraveled. In Wisconsin the center sometimes appears to have wandered off and gotten irretrievably lost.

Last summer I may have located the center if by "center" you mean a middle ground of agreement between diverse parties. I had gone up near Lake Superior to teach a course in memoir writing to people who were nothing if not diverse: a CEO, a corporate attorney, a psychiatrist, a veterinarian, some retired teachers, even a forester—men and women in their fifties and sixties who, having navigated most of life's curves, now wanted to write about the experience. Since conflict is the engine that runs most narratives, it wasn't surprising that many of the memoirs dealt with one calamity or another. The only young person taking the class, a high school student who needed a few credits to graduate, must have wondered why so many of the stories he was hearing from his elders turned on alcoholic parents or physical abuse or hard times in general.

Surprisingly, the one conflict that never came up that week was politics. Maybe the people in the class were just being polite or felt isolated from the latest news cycle or maybe, looking back over the years, they realized that the *sturm und drang* of party politics seems pretty trivial set against the real drama of people's lives.

At week's end, the class read their memoirs aloud. When it was the high school student's turn, we all wondered what could possibly cloud such a short, seemingly perfect life. Bright and ridiculously handsome, the young man said what we'd expected, that school came easy for him but his last semester had turned out to be a real bummer. Nothing actually happened except that he'd begun to have terrible doubts about the sort of world he was soon to enter. Judging from the news, he said in a faltering voice, it was an awful place—filled with war and wrangling and hate. What was the point?

Like so many stricken aunts and uncles, we assured the young man that he was wrong. The world is a fine place, we told him. There may be troubles aplenty in it, but they aren't all yours. Face the ones that are and try to enjoy yourself. The rest is just politics.

Weasel

HAVING MANEUVERED as quietly as possible through a black-berry thicket in the freezing dark to reach a narrow ridge, I spent the rest of the morning not seeing deer. What I did see was a black comma shape advancing in fits and starts up the ridge. In hunting, the trick is to look not for the quarry but for movement and then let the animal fill in around it. When the comma stopped moving, the rest of it took shape: a lithe, slender body, pure white except for a pair of obsidian eyes and the black tip of a tail. It was the tail I'd been seeing all along, and it belonged to a weasel. I'd never seen one before in winter phase. Perfectly camouflaged against the snow, the weasel had been hunting that morning as well, and more successfully; a limp mouse dangled from its mouth like a bit of gray scarf. The weasel stopped at the base of a tall ash tree. Then it ran straight up the trunk, stuffed the mouse into a knothole, and disappeared inside as well, the tip of its black tail the last to go.

Why do I remember that weasel so many years after it vanished into the knothole? Why should someone so terrible at putting names to faces recall a chance encounter with a small mammal when I can't remember my own neighbors, let alone those who've borrowed tools and haven't returned them?

It's not just the weasel occupying space in my prefrontal cortex. There's a hissing otter that once followed my canoe down the White River. And a young badger that appeared and disappeared as I was unloading a boat near its hidden den. These encounters remain hard-coded into my memory probably because they never occurred on my terms. They were brief and surprising and seemed like meaningful visitations—if I could just figure out what they meant.

Animal stories from childhood lead us to expect a world varied in its wonders and yet strangely accessible because the tigers and bears that inhabit them act as metaphors for our own behavior. My favorite storybook character was Rikki-tikki-tavi, the brave little mongoose from Kipling's *The Jungle Book,* who saves the sahib's children from a pair of wicked cobras. Postcolonialists would probably call Rikki an imperialist stooge today, but to me he was the essence of a selfless hero. The point is that real animals are neither brave nor cruel but simply themselves, and whatever human qualities we recognize in them are simply projections of something latent in ourselves.

The weasel I saw in the November woods was surprisingly unweasely in its behavior; its approach was nothing if not direct. After our encounter, I knew I'd have to find another metaphor for cunning manipulation, one closer to home.

What animals represent best these days is their own species. A wildlife biologist might differentiate between individuals, but for most of us an encounter with an animal in the wild is so rare that the individual comes to stand for the entire population. Not *a* weasel but *the* weasel. That's how I first thought about animals as a child. My family used to visit an uncle's cottage on a lake that wasn't wild but had a shallow, weedy lagoon at one end. Every evening at dusk we'd gather by the picture window to watch a large wading bird stalk frogs among the lagoon's cattails. The bird was taller than I was and managed to look regal and angry at the same time. *What's that?* I asked. When the answer came, *the Great Blue Heron,* I remember the thrill of seeing such a legendary figure, first and last of its kind.

DECEMBER

Skating Backwards

LAST YEAR my hometown announced it was mothballing most of the neighborhood ice skating rinks, ours included. A city crew would no longer flood the rinks on successive freezing nights or pay listless teenagers to sit in overheated warming huts or break up hockey games that spilled into the main rink. Budget cuts was the reason given, though there were also a string of freakishly warm winters and a general decline in use. As a consolation prize, a few larger ice rinks remain open, but I miss the one in our neighborhood, the one we could walk to, the one where my children learned to skate. It's one more instance of the landscape of childhood giving way to that notoriously poor substitute: memory.

But whose memory? One of the weird pleasures of parenthood is making children reenact some tableau from your own childhood. And nothing is rigged with déjà vu like a skating rink at night. It's one big memory sink: the dome of darkness overhead, the scuffle of skates, the way everything shimmers in the cold night air. All that sensory input can't help but trigger a lightning storm of synapses in the brain.

One persistent memory I have is of skating flawlessly backwards with a girl under the lights. It's a school night and I've been dropped at the city rink. Snow is falling heavily out of a blackness that begins just beyond the arc lights. And there's music! The entire rink revolves slowly on its axis as a loudspeaker blares "The Skater's Waltz." Among those orbiting past is a girl I recognize from class, someone I've never spoken to but whose mere presence elicits a strange new excitement. She's wearing a nubby blue sweater and short woolen skirt that's left her bare legs red in the cold. I push off, weaving between skaters, until she's just ahead, trailing a fragrance that's equal parts wool, freshly washed hair, and spearmint chewing gum. With a few powerful strokes I glide past her and then—amazing!—pivot so we're face to face, skating in perfect rhythm as she smiles and offers up her arms.

Except it never happened. I didn't learn to skate backwards until I was in my thirties, so the whole episode is a false memory, a hiccup in the temporal lobe, a scene concocted out of adolescent longing or something I must have read. When I finally learned that by wriggling my skates toe-in and toe-out I could move in reverse across the ice, the knowledge came too late for me to play hockey or meet girls as a teenager but in plenty of time for me to teach my own kids to skate.

"They'll never learn *that* way!" a babysitter once complained, pointing to the kids' double-runner skates.

She was right. You can't grasp the Newtonian physics of skating—pushing backwards on one foot to slide forward on the other—until you can balance on knife-edge blades. So I bought real skates—white for her, black for him—and held the kids' hands while skating backwards across the ice, a stable outrigger for their rubbery ankles. When they got the hang of it, I let go. And they kept gliding over the years—on bicycles, cars, transatlantic flights—until they eventually sailed out of sight.

Now on winter nights my wife and I drive to one of the rinks still open and circle the ice in an approximation of a waltz. If this looks romantic from a distance, it's only because you can't see the stagecraft—the hand-squeezing that signals a turn or the way we keep time by humming the brutal cadence of "The Skater's

Waltz"—*Dah-dah Dah-DUM! Dah-dah Dah-DUM!*—while alternately pushing and pulling each other around the rink. It's not dancing so much as balancing, a kind of novelty act, marriage on ice. Still, when we lock arms and go into a spin, faster and faster, and everything blurs together except her astonished blue eyes, and I'll think: *This must be love.*

Deer at Twilight

AT TWILIGHT, four of us sat knee-to-knee on overturned buckets in a small camouflage blind watching a snowy stubble field turned milky blue. After a half hour a pair of deer drifted out of the surrounding birch and began feeding. They alternated postures of hunger and alertness, lowering their heads to feed, then abruptly looking up, as if they sensed that a pile of shelled corn in the middle of a stubble field was no accident. Christopher Jacques, a DNR research scientist, had spread the corn at the base of a flagpole supporting a 40 x 60 nylon drop-net. The burly and bearded Jacques (pronounced Jakes) had written his PhD dissertation on pronghorn antelope in South Dakota before heading up a long-term study of Wisconsin's whitetails. He hardly seemed to notice as more deer floated out of the woods. Soon there were nearly a dozen whitetails in the stubble field, and I thought surely one would notice the orange extension cord running from the flagpole to our blind.

We'd spent the morning driving back roads in the Flambeau River State Forest and checking box traps to see if they held any deer. The problem with box traps is that they catch raccoons and crows, as well as deer who've already been radio-collared. One enormous buck had been captured four times before the box trap was finally moved. A drop-net is more selective. But watching deer unseen from a blind can feel like surveillance, like a prelude to a drug bust.

Some of the deer began evaporating back into the woods. Finally, when only three does remained beneath the net, Jacques nodded and one of the women in the crew touched the lead wires from the extension cord to a pair of battery terminals. The net dropped and we all started running.

By the time I reached the net, last and out of breath, the largest deer had wriggled free and pogo-sticked into the night. Jacques had one doe on the ground and the women had the other. He suggested we switch places. So he slid off the doe as I slid on, straddling her to keep my weight evenly distributed and my head to one side in case she bucked. She didn't move but kept up a hoarse, panicky bleating until Jacques slipped a red blindfold over her eyes. Then the doe quieted down and the only sound was heavy breathing, hers and mine. This was the closest I'd ever gotten to a deer, a living one, at any rate.

Jacques has three rules for handling live-trapped deer: No unnecessary talking. No putting weight on the animal's head. And no petting. When I'd asked Jacques why he didn't want people petting the deer, he said curtly, "Because they don't like it."

But that's exactly what I wanted to do. My hands sunk deep into brindled fur, I felt the doe's rib cage accordion in and out and wished there was some way to assure her that my intentions were harmless. It wouldn't have mattered. Everything about deer—their semaphore ears, wide-set eyes, long legs, frenetic birthrate—evolved as a response to predators. So with lights out and a heavy body splayed across her back, how could the doe not conclude that I was anything but another predator—which, of course, is what I am.

I'd volunteered to assist in the DNR's long-term deer study because I hunt in the study's northern forest area, a heavily wooded region with few roads and a full slate of predators—gray wolves, black bears, coyotes, bobcats. And while I couldn't know what the doe was thinking, it was easy to imagine a predator's mindset— a wolf or coyote that's run its prey to ground, the deer's body thumping alive beneath it, the lifeblood soon to augment its own.

Radiotelemetry studies like this one are designed to show what effect predation has on the state's deer herd. Last year predators of every stripe killed ten radio-collared adult and yearling deer in the northern study zone—half as many as hunters. Yet wolves have largely taken the blame from hunters and politicians who've vowed to make the North Woods safe for venison. Nearly all the recovered radio collars from the study were returned by hunters at deer registration stations. Others showed evidence of poaching, like the collar found hanging in a tree or the one still transmitting from the North Fork of the Flambeau River where it had been tossed from a highway bridge. What the study has shown so far is that deer lead complex lives. They're the fulcrum where human intentions and the needs of other species come together and occasionally clash. It's hard to see our role in all this with any objectivity.

The moon was up as the crew rolled up the net to work on the doe. The women took measurements and a blood sample and fixed a radio collar around the doe's neck so they could track her movements and know if she stopped moving altogether. Then Jacques told me to slide to one side and leave a clear exit to the woods. When I did, the doe bolted. We could hear her crashing through the dark for a long time and then nothing.

Vernacular

MY FATHER-IN-LAW called the obituary page in the newspaper the "Irish Sporting News" and threatened to "put the kibosh" on ill-considered projects, whatever that meant. If a chain slipped while he was pulling fence posts or a steer we'd run through a squeeze chute turned out later to be a bull, the worst he might say was "Christ O'Friday!" Where did those words come from? What did they mean? I don't know, but they're so linked in my mind with the speaker that it was his gravelly voice I heard, not mine, when I said them in a eulogy at his funeral mass. The officiating priest shot me a quick glance.

My father-in-law was a third-generation farmer who never left the home place apart from a brief stint flying in the Pacific. He'd eat "dinner" at midday then drive "over east" to check his cattle before returning in the evening for "supper." But most of his idioms were rooted in time rather than place. When he admonished a grandchild to "straighten up and fly right," I thought it was something he, the ex-pilot, had made up himself until I heard the Andrew Sisters crooning it on an old time radio show.

A shared language is a form of belonging as well as a way of distinguishing insiders from outsiders. When strangers asked permission to hunt the farm, they'd sometimes fall into a "yokel" accent, dropping their g's and *jes wonderin' if ya seen any bucks over t' holler.* My father-in-law never talked that way and must have wondered why anyone would imitate a dialect nobody spoke. The biggest difference I've noticed between the way people speak in the country as opposed to the city is more in the pauses between words than the words themselves. A two-beat pause can be a way of defusing an obvious disaster. Once, after digging a cattle hauler out of the snow so he could deliver a load of bred heifers, we watched one of the heifers crash through the corral fence and hightail it across the pasture. I asked my father-in-law if we ought to give chase. "No," he said, doing a slow burn. "I think we've had enough fun for one day."

Time more than geography is the great divider of the way we talk. In 1940, when E.B. White wrote "Maine Speech," he identified dozens of Down East-isms distinguished by their regionalized meaning, pronunciation, or grammar. I wonder how many he'd find now. My list for the Upper Midwest is short: "bubblers" and "brats" and the annoying Germanic habit of dropping the object of the preposition when asking someone if they want to "come with." We still flatten our vowels so the consonants won't feel neglected, but I'd love to hear what Midwesterners sounded like before TV and sports radio ratcheted up the dialogue.

Of course, there's no "place" in the country where language is off the grid. The closest I've come is a reel-to-reel tape-recording made at my grandparents' Chicago apartment on Christmas Day 1952. It was made by an uncle remembered for his big, boxy recording machine the way another uncle was known for his musical car horn. By the time I inherited it, the recording was in terrible shape; the acetate was gone in places and some of the breaks had been spliced together with masking tape. I took it to a sound engineer who repaired the splices and made a master in his studio while I listened with headphones.

At first there's only the waterfall roar of wrapping paper being torn from presents; then a face floats like a balloon up from time's airshaft tied to the thin, wavering voice of Aunt Kathleen, a voice punctuated by her smoker's hack. There is no talk of the greater world, of the war in Korea, or of Eisenhower's recent thumping of Stevenson. Instead the adults drink coffee, wonder if the heat's been turned on, express false surprise at every gift my brothers and I tear into. City dwellers, they speak with the slow deliberation we associate with the country, unhurried and without inflection as if they had all the time in the world. The only hyper voices belong to my brothers and me, jabbering pipsqueaks who sound as if we'd taken hits off a helium balloon.

"Oh boy, I got a stocking! I got a stocking!" my older brother shouts as if he'd never been through this before.

The person I'm waiting to hear most is absent for the first few minutes, away on some errand, until a door swings open and my father steps across the threshold of years. Sadly, his is the only voice I don't immediately recognize because I haven't heard it since I was seven. In a real sense, this is the first time I've heard him speak. Like listeners at a séance, we want the dead to speak to us directly, to say something of importance across the years. Instead they make small talk or, in my father's case, read in all seriousness a gag gift from my brother, something called a Fur-O-Meter.

"If tail is dry . . . fair. If tail is wet . . . rain. If tail is frosty . . . cold. If tail is gone . . . cyclone."

Caught in the moment, the dead don't share our sense of its poignancy now that the moment is gone—which is part of their charm. Halfway through the gift opening the tape abruptly jumps tracks to a party that evening at my grandparents' apartment. For once adults drown out the children with a deep, rolling swell of after-dinner chatter. The men are in shirtsleeves on the sofa, the women clearing the table; a heavy cloud of cigar smoke tinged with lilac water hangs in the air. Uncle Eddie sounds like a tough guy in the movies as he rues the second-hand Buick he bought instead of a Lincoln and gripes that his boss treats him like "some guy to lug his grip."

As the party winds down, people struggle into coats and hats, bracing themselves for the cold. But before they leave, the tape recorder uncle passes around the microphone and instructs everyone to impart a holiday greeting, something for posterity. And for whom are these greetings intended if not ourselves tucked safely in the future? Except for my grandfather, who does a turn as a stage Irishman, the others sign off as more or less themselves. "Merry Christmas and many more," warbles Aunt Florence. One by one they make their farewells and slip quietly into the night until only Aunt Marcella remains. "It's been a nice party, but it's time to go," she sighs as if turning out a light.

Long Night's Journey

THE TWO-HOUR DRIVE HOME from my in-laws' farm feels longer at midwinter than it did three months ago even though I leave at exactly the same time. That's because I've been racing the sun—or rather Earth's tilt away from the sun—since midsummer and steadily losing ground. Between Thanksgiving and Christmas, I've lost a half hour of daylight, which is the difference between crossing the bridge at Wabasha and seeing a river as opposed to a darker seam of darkness.

It's not just *the* days that seem shortened by winter but *my* days, so much that the sunrise-sunset chart in the newspaper begins to look like an actuarial table. There are biological reasons for feeling gloomy: prolonged darkness decreases the level of mood-enhancing serotonin in the brain while increasing amounts of melatonin, the same hormone that causes bears to hibernate.

The good news is the way the darkness frames the light makes us notice its sheer variability, or as Theodore Roethke wrote, "In a dark time, the eye begins to see." For one thing, darkness doesn't fall like a final curtain as the sun dips below the horizon. It's more like a dimmer switch with four separate settings. Driving east, I see the first stage, "sunset twilight," as a bar of louvered light climbing the side of a barn. Snowfields go from white to salmon-pink and then an icy blue. Sometime between "civil" and "nautical twilight," the moon rises high enough to turn the countryside into negative image of itself. And by the final stage, "astronomical twilight," our car is rocketing beneath a slot of sky that's become outer space.

Farmhouses sail past in the dark. Sometimes a face is framed in a window, though more often than not there's only a flickering blue light, the one that wires us to the same waking dreams and makes the night feel even emptier. Between Durand and Rock Falls I pass a scattering of Amish farmhouses. In daylight I can tell they're Amish by the horses in the yard or the row of frozen bloomers pegged to a clothesline. But at night the windows give them away. Glazed in a thin, yellow light, they're like sepia photographs in an old family album. The rooms are spare and mostly empty; all I can really see is walls, and yet looking in those passing windows is like looking into the nineteenth century, when houses were lit by kerosene lanterns and waking dreams weren't interrupted by commercials.

The Christmas decorations have mostly come down in the small towns along the way except for a plywood Santa Claus waiting forlornly in one front yard as if for a bus. In the long-ago of my children's childhood, we always spent one winter night driving around to look at Christmas lights. Our own neighborhood tended toward electric candles in windows or a string of icicle lights along the eaves—tasteful but boring. The most garish, eye-popping, Las Vegas-meets-the-Nativity light displays were inevitably on the outskirts of town where people felt less deterred by neighbors or maybe more overwhelmed by darkness.

"It's a beauty!" our youngest daughter would announce after each gaudy show of colored lights until it became a running joke, the family punch line to any unexpected sight that livened up a dull trip.

There's a long stretch of darkness along the last few miles before we crest a hill and spot the electric glare above the city. It's light pollution, visible no doubt from outer space, and a terrible waste of energy. Still, I'm always happy to see the sky aglow after a long night's journey, heartened that so many neighbors left their lights on to show us the way home.

As we say, *it's a beauty.*

Acknowledgments

Most of these essays originally appeared, sometimes in different form, in *Wisconsin Trails* magazine, and I owe the editors there—Harriet Brown, Kristen Scheuing, Chelsey Lewis—a debt of gratitude. I'd also like to thank Kate Thompson, who brought those pieces together as a book. Finally, thanks to my wife, Sharon, whose thoughts, experiences, and good advice I've plundered at will.

About the Author

Photo by Sharon Hildebrand

JOHN HILDEBRAND is the author of the award-winning books *A Northern Front: New & Selected Essays, Mapping the Farm: The Chronicle of a Family,* and *Reading the River: A Voyage Down the Yukon.* His work has appeared in such magazines as *Harper's, Audubon, Sports Illustrated,* and *Outside.* He teaches at the University of Wisconsin–Eau Claire and divides his time between home and a cabin in northern Wisconsin.